THE TEARS OF MY SOUL

There are some stories which seem so far from reality that they stop you cold. Such is the story of Sokreaksa. However, even with all of its tragedy, it moves the reader into the realm of healing and wholeness. A first-century story for a twenty-first-century heart. (Dr Brian C. Stiller, President, Tyndale University College & Seminary)

This book provides a terribly poignant glimpse into the life of one "ordinary" Cambodian who suffered and survived the horrific genocide of the Pol Pot regime. It is the deeply moving first-person account of the grace and mercy of God in and through the life of one brutally battered survivor whose wrenching experiences and deep personal loss have been sanctified for the Master's use. The author and his family now serve as missionaries in Cambodia, incarnating the love and forgiveness of God for those who destroyed his family and attempted to destroy him. This short book is a reminder of the transforming power of the Gospel, and it is MUST reading. (Jonathan J. Bonk, Executive Director, Overseas Ministries Study Center, Connecticut)

As Sokreaksa climbs the mountain of the Lord, he arrives, as all the saints do, at a place of sacrifice. There he discovers that God himself has been this way before him. *Tears of my Soul* points the way for a nation, on its knees, searching for absolution. (Don Cormack, author of *Killing Fields, Living Fields*)

The searing story of one man's journey from horror, suffering and loss to freedom, faith and new purpose. Compelling and uplifting reading. (Peter Lewis, Cornerstone Evangelical Church, Nottingham)

In my years of teaching at Providence Theological Seminary, I was frequently aware of my unworthiness to address the topics of forgiveness and pain for some students. This was especially true when Sokreaksa Himm was in class. No one who has lived in North America knows what it is to forgive the pain experienced on the killing fields of Cambodia. Helmut Thieleke has said America does not have an adequate theology of pain. This story will fill a theological gap which Christians and churches in this country cannot address in the same way. (A. H. Konkel, Providence College and Seminary, Otterburne, Manitoba)

The Tears of My Soul

He survived Cambodia's killing fields.
His family didn't. Could he forgive?

SOKREAKSA S. HIMM
with
JAN GREENOUGH

MONARCH
BOOKS

Oxford, UK & Grand Rapids, Michigan, USA

First published in the UK in 2003 by Monarch Books (a publishing imprint of
Lion Hudson plc), Mayfield House, 256 Banbury Road, Oxford OX2 7DH.
Tel: +44 (0)1865 302750 Fax: +44 (0)1865 302757
Email: monarch@lionhudson.com
www.lionhudson.com

Reprinted 2003, 2005, 2006

ISBN-13: 978-1-85424-612-7 (UK)
ISBN-10: 1-85424-612-7 (UK)
ISBN-13: 978-0-8254-6218-4 (USA)
ISBN-10: 0-8254-6218-5 (USA)

Distributed by:
UK: Marston Book Services Ltd, PO Box 269,
Abingdon, Oxon OX14 4YN;
USA: Kregel Publications, PO Box 2607,
Grand Rapids, Michigan 49501

British Library Cataloguing Data
A catalogue record for this book is available from the British Library.

Printed and bound in Great Britain by Cox & Wyman Ltd, Reading.

CONTENTS

ACKNOWLEDGEMENTS

This space is insufficient for me to express my thanks to those who deserve it. But most of all I would like to thank God the Father, the Son and the Holy Spirit. Without his protection and care, I would not have had the chance to write this book.

The following people have ministered to me in many different ways:

Especially, my beloved sister Sopheap Himm who has always encouraged me to keep living and to persevere. She is the best person, and I have grieved with her for years. She has been willing to suffer alongside me. Without her emotional support I would not have been able to survive. My foster father, Mov, who endangered his life to save me when I was being persecuted.

My lovely wife, Sophaly Eng, and my son, Philos Reaksa Himm, who have brought great joy to my life. They have fulfilled the longing in my heart.

My foster mother, Carolyn Ulrich, who has sincerely loved me as her own son and supported me emotionally while I was suffering from depression.

Dr Sorpong Poeu, Pastor James Bo, and his wife Sakhoeun Thai, who have always encouraged me to love Jesus, to desire his word, and to seek first his kingdom.

Chuck Ferguson who shared Jesus' love and forgiveness with me when I arrived in Canada. He is the friend who has brought me hope and the joy of life.

Rudy Dirks and his family who have accepted and loved me as a member of their family.

Khun Lam and Loeuy Tan who motivated and encouraged me to pursue my higher education.

I also wish to acknowledge Dr Alan Kirk, Dr Jon Bonk, Dr Gus Konkel and Elizabeth Davey who have read my manuscript patiently and given me some guidelines. I particularly wish to thank Jan Greenough for her compassionate and creative editorial work. Professor Dr Chuck Nichols, Professor Dr Larry Dixon, John Franklin, Mary Houghe, Gerry T. Neal and Conrad James Lee have prayed for me and exhorted me to walk through the pain. Rev. Dr Duc X Nguyen, Dr David Cochran, Dr William Craigs, Dr Nancy Craigs, Phil Ulrich, Chung's family, Evelyn Armstrong, Layswan Goh, Dr William Wan and Isobel Crites all prayed for me and supported me financially and emotionally when I was doing my undergraduate and graduate studies.

Finally, I would like to thank Ramsay Chan's family, Wayne Duesling's family, Cerintha Chia, Rebecca Lee, Pak Soon Lau, Neel and Pam Reynolds, Alvin Dah, Ron Terry, Dr Brian Stiller, Margaret Gilligan and Dr Grover Crosby who have encouraged me to see the glory of serving the Lord in my homeland.

Finally, I would like to thank Pieter Kwant, John Wallis and Ivor Greer who have helped me to get this book published.

These people have done great things for me, and I owe them much.

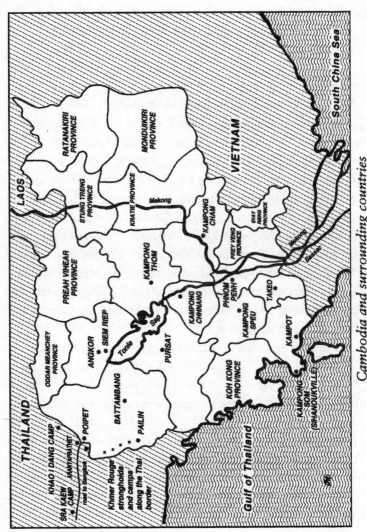

Cambodia and surrounding countries

PREFACE

In 1990, in my first class at Ontario Bible College (now Tyndale College), I was asked to introduce myself. I told my classmates a little about myself and where I came from. They seemed confused about Cambodia. One of the students asked, "Where is Cambodia?" I had a little difficulty telling him. I asked, "Have you ever heard about Kampuchea?" His response was "no". "Have you ever seen Angkor Wat?" "No." "Have you ever heard about the killing fields?" He did not answer me and I could tell that he was frustrated by my questions. As I discovered, Cambodia is not well known in Canada.

Cambodia, in southeast Asia, was once known as "The Land of Paradise". Most of the Khmer, or Kampuchean, people led a peaceful, harmonious existence cultivating rice in the countryside. In the past five decades, however, Cambodia has been turned upside-down. In 1941 Prince Norodom Sihanouk became king, and managed to bring the country to full independence by 1953. One year after that he relinquished his throne to his father, and entered the political arena. Later, he became the prime minister and head of state. During this time, he tried to keep Cambodia out of the war being fought in neighboring countries. He seemed reasonably successful in dealing with the external political pressure, but he failed to manage the internal political factor. Internally, he was opposed by both the leftist Khmer Rouge (Red Khmer or Khmer Communist) led by Pol Pot, and by the rightists (his own government).

In early 1970, the king was overthrown and the monarchy abolished. A Khmer republic was established, led by General Lon Nol and supported by the Americans. Sihanouk went to China, where he decided to ally himself with his former enemy the Khmer Rouge, to try to regain control of Cambodia. He became the head of state for the Khmer Rouge, but he had no actual power over the Khmer Rouge soldiers.

Between 1970 and 1975 civil war raged throughout Cambodia. The country was gradually engulfed by the Khmer Rouge soldiers, and the government of the republic grew totally corrupt. The society became chaotic. Many who hated corruption were psychologically coerced into joining the Khmer Rouge to fight the government of the republic. In April 1975, the Khmer Rouge captured the whole country.

Soon after the Khmer Rouge took over, they turned Cambodia into the "Land of Killing Fields". People were evacuated from the cities to work in the countryside. Life under the Khmer Rouge's merciless regime became meaningless and worthless. My family was one of the innocent families forced to do hard labour with little food to eat. In 1977, my family was executed by the Khmer Rouge. I, along with my sister, survived the killing. During the reign of the Khmer Rouge, it is estimated that two million Cambodian people were killed.

In early 1979 Cambodia came under another regime, this one supported by the Vietnamese government. In late 1984, I escaped to a refugee camp in Thailand where I stayed for five years. In 1989, I was accepted for resettlement in the "Land of Opportunity" – Canada. This book is the true story of my unheard crying in the Khmer Rouge brutal regime and my life after I witnessed the killing of my family and came to Christ.

Reaksa S. Himm
January 2003

DEDICATION

This book is affectionately dedicated to the memory of:

1. My father Soeum Himm
2. My mother Kimcheav Ry
3. My eldest brother Sophoan Himm
4. My elder brother Pinith Himm
5. My elder brother Piney Himm
6. My elder sister Sopheavy Himm
7. My younger brother Sokmeth Himm
8. My younger brother Sopheak Himm
9. My youngest sister Somaly Himm
10. My younger brother Sophat Himm
11. My youngest brother Thlok Phirounn Himm
12. My sister-in-law Sophanny Sar
13. My nephew Sophoan Himm Jr

who were killed in 1977 under the Khmer Rouge regime.

CHAPTER ONE

EVACUATION

"There is a road, but no people are walking on it. There is a house, but no people are living in it." Cambodian saying.

It was 17th April 1975: the day the Khmer Communists made history with their great victory over capitalism. Five years of civil war in Cambodia had come to an end, and General Lon Nol's republican regime, supported by the United States, was overthrown. The Khmer Rouge army had been gradually taking over towns and villages across the country, and with the fall of the capital, Phnom Penh, after four months of heavy bombardment, their victory was complete. They had fought against the American troops, never giving up in spite of their lack of weapons, and they had finally kicked these troops out of the country.

At this point every Cambodian thought the war was over; they thought there would be *santrane*, or "peace". Cambodians would live peacefully as they had for centuries, the sounds of war would disappear and life would be prosperous. But *santrane* never came. The peaceful land of the Khmer Rouge propaganda was turned into killing fields, ploughed with chaos and suffering.

A few days after they claimed victory over the Americans, the Khmer Rouge invited all those who had been associated with the republican government to appear before the *angkar loeu* (which means "higher organisation"). Politicians, military officers and government officials were all summoned: they were told they had to study the communist doctrines of the new regime if they were to co-operate with the *angkar loeu* in the future. All these people were anxious to retain their positions of authority, so they reported as requested, but they never came back. All were killed. The Khmer Communists used the words "study" or "go to school" as a euphemism for execution.

This was the people's first taste of the brutal mentality of the Khmer Rouge, and it was incomprehensible. Everyone thought the *angkar* could be trusted absolutely; they had promised peace. The people who died were highly educated, but they had fallen into a simple trap and given themselves up voluntarily for execution. No one could believe that the Khmer Rouge would kill people, or that they would turn the "land of paradise" into killing fields.

The execution of the intellectuals was only the beginning. Not long after, the Khmer Rouge came calling at every house in Siemreap city, where I lived with my family. They said that the *angkar loeu* believed that there were still American soldiers in hiding, and that they must be routed out. Therefore, could they respectfully invite the people to leave for just three days, so that the Khmer Rouge would have a chance to clean the city properly? Since we were leaving for only three days, we wouldn't need to take all our belongings with us. The *angkar loeu* would be personally responsible for any missing property, which we could claim whenever we came back. Just prepare enough food for three days. And so we did.

I was eleven years old, and I had lived most of my life in Siemreap; I was born in Pouk district, about ten miles away. We were a close-knit family: my parents, three brothers and two sisters older than me, and three brothers and a sister younger. (My youngest brother Thlok was born after the evacuation.) When I woke up the next morning my parents were already packing. My older brothers and sisters were planning to take only a few clothes, some food and some medicines, but my father was worried. "Why should the *angkar* want to evacuate a whole city for only three days?" he said. "It's a huge undertaking." He knew something of the communist mentality: their propaganda spoke of the dignity of labour and the value of the peasants. He suspected that the *angkar loeu* were going to send all city-dwellers to live in the jungle or work on the farms, and would never let us come back home. He told us to pack as much as we could, including fishing equipment and gardening tools. We weren't sure why our father felt like this – taking farming equipment with us was against the instructions of the Khmer Rouge – but we obeyed him anyway and collected what we thought could be useful. Our neighbours laughed at us: they thought our family was stupid to carry all this useless luggage.

My eldest brother, Sophoan, was engaged to a young woman called Sophanny Sar, and he was desperate not to be separated from her. In all the chaos of the evacuation, how would they ever find each other? He went to my father and asked permission to bring Sophanny along with our family. It wasn't usual for an engaged couple to do this, but these weren't usual times, and my father agreed. Sophoan went and collected her at once. I'd never seen Sophanny before, and I was rather in awe of her: she was very beautiful. My mother liked her very much, but her happiness was tinged with sorrow that Sophoan wouldn't be able to get married in the traditional manner. We could do nothing more, yet nothing better, than welcome her with joy into our family.

My father was proved right: when we arrived at the

appointed place we saw Khmer Rouge soldiers forcing people to evacuate the city. We were shocked to see what was happening; every street was crowded with dazed people carrying their bags, amazed at the rough treatment they were getting from the "liberating" soldiers. All around us, people were crying bitterly. Some had got separated from their families and were wandering around looking for their relatives. Sick people had been forced out of the hospitals and many of them lay dying by the roadside. It was a scene of chaos. My father told us to stay close together and be prepared for anything.

We were forced to get into a military truck. We tried to carry on board as much as we could, but a soldier saw how much we were carrying, and threw some of our bags out onto the road. One of them was a bag of my clothes, and I jumped down to get it just as the truck was starting up. As I bent to retrieve it, I felt something cold on the back of my head: it was the muzzle of a gun.

"Leave it!" barked the soldier. "Get in the truck!"

I was terrified. My father and my sister were shouting at me to leave the bag and get in. I was angry but there was nothing I could do, so I straightened up, trembling, and climbed into the truck. The family grabbed me and held me tightly, and as the truck pulled away I looked back at my bag lying in the middle of the road.

As we travelled westward everyone was trying to comfort me after my fright. What if the soldier had pulled the trigger? For the first time I understood how fragile life was – I could have died in that moment. I'd never realised how deeply my mother loved me till I saw her face: she was terrified of losing me.

After half an hour we arrived at Pouk district, where we were ordered off the truck. Now at last we had a chance to talk, and to be introduced properly to Sophanny. We boys were full of admiration for our eldest brother for finding such a beautiful wife. We planned to hold their wedding at the next stop, if time permitted: Sophoan and Sophanny couldn't live together without getting married according to the traditional rites, but with everything turned upside down, nothing could be done about it now.

We waited around for three hours before we got the order to leave again. Thirty or forty lorries arrived and took us on to the western part of Siemreap province. At sunset, we arrived at a village called Chinlease Thay, about forty miles from Siemreap city. We had to stop there for the night: the drivers would go no further because the road had been severely damaged in the war, and there were still a lot of mines in the ground. It would be very dangerous to drive there in the dark.

There, at Chinlease Thay village, we married our eldest brother to his fiancée. We had enough food to eat and so our dinner was their wedding party, and they were pronounced husband and wife. It was a very sad wedding for Sophoan and his wife, but it was the best we could do in that chaotic situation. They spent their wedding night right there with us, on the ground. When they woke up the next morning, they were upset to see two graves close by: to spend one's honeymoon beside a grave was surely a bad omen.

That morning we were ordered to move on again. This time the lorries took us north-west, and about three o'clock we arrived at Chrouyneang Ngoun village. This was a temporary stopping place, the main centre for the Phnom Sreysnom district. Only a few Khmer Rouge soldiers were there to direct operations. I had no idea how they managed to disperse such large numbers of people to so many different places, or how their communication system functioned, but I could see that they were well organised.

We stayed there for another two weeks. It was very hard for us: April, May and June are very hot in Cambodia, we were not used to sleeping on the ground, and all of us were squeezed into a very small tent. However, we tried to adapt as well as we could, for otherwise we knew what would happen. Already the Khmer Rouge soldiers were stepping up the psychological and emotional pressure. A few evacuees from the city hadn't brought enough food, medicine or other necessities for the hot season, and they complained about the conditions we were forced to live in. They accused the *angkar* of betrayal, lying to us about the evacuation, forcing us from our homes and taking us so far from the city. Their punishment was immediate: they were arrested, taken into the jungle and killed. It was a warning to us all. To complain was to rebel, and anyone who rebelled against the *angkar loeu* would be killed. They didn't call it that, of course. They said that anyone who rebelled would have to learn their lesson: they would be taken into the jungle "to study". Whenever they said those words, or talked about being "sent to school", we were paralysed with fear. We knew what it meant.

As for the Khmer Rouge soldiers, we called them "The Black Evils", because they all wore black clothes. We never saw them as human beings: it seemed to us that they were filled with evil spirits.

Life took on a certain routine. We were provided with rice and salt, but no clean water – our only water came from a polluted pond. A few years earlier, during a battle with the Khmer Rouge, two republican soldiers had been killed and their bodies dumped there. Now we drank from it, not knowing about the corpses in the water. The skeletons and uniforms of the soldiers were found later.

We were told that this clearing in the forest was where we were going to live, so we had to build our own house. We all helped build a shelter big enough for the family, cutting down young trees to make stilts to raise the floor above the flood water in the rainy season, using palm leaves to thatch the roof and making beds from bamboo. Then we dug the ground around the house to plant vegetables, corn, potatoes and rice. We were glad we'd brought the gardening tools, and that we'd managed to hang on to the nets and lines for catching fish. We'd never been in such a situation before, but thanks to my father's foresight we were reasonably well prepared. Life was going to be hard, but we were determined to survive. We did whatever the *angkar* told us to, because we wanted to live.

Once we'd built our settlement in the jungle, the place was given a new name: "New-Liberated Village" or "17th April Village". Literally, it meant that the people in this village had been liberated from capitalism on the day of the Khmer Rouge victory. It was the same all over the country: the people in the countryside had been "liberated" first, and by now some of the rural communities had been living under communist rule for several years. The cities, which were the last to fall, were then emptied systematically, and the people forced into the country-side as we had been, to be "purified" through labour. As inhab-itants of the cities which had resisted the Khmer Rouge we were automatically assumed to be capitalist supporters of the Americans. Now we, too, had been "liberated" to serve the *angkar loeu* and our country, but we were the "new-liberated" – marked out as capitalist collaborators – and as such inferior to the "old-liberated" rural peasants and farmers. This distinc-tion was to rule our lives for the next few years.

The Khmer Rouge had been incredibly well organised: hun-dreds of families like us were sent into the jungle to build their own segregated settlements. Who were the ones chosen for exile? First they chose the families of soldiers, policemen and administrators of the former republic; they also sent away anyone who was Chinese. Then they selected all the profes-sors, teachers and students. My father was a teacher, so we were sent to live in the jungle of Reusey Sagn with two hundred other teachers' families.

The idea of the segregation was to put us under pressure. They forced us to live separately from the old-liberated people to see if we, with our "intellectual" abilities, could survive in the jungle. We were completely powerless and helpless – the prisoners of the Khmer Rouge, although not in jail. We couldn't go anywhere without their permission, and our every action had to conform to their rules, otherwise we would be punished or "sent to study". In effect, the jungle had become both a physical and psychological prison.

To keep a tight hold on the population, the Khmer Rouge leaders relied heavily on informers. They encouraged people to dedicate themselves enthusiastically to the communist cause, and promoted some to be group leaders or *chlops* (a kind of secret agent, investigator or soldier, but who did not carry a gun or rifle). They never chose educated people for this work: they selected the poorest of the peasantry, mostly illiterate, who wouldn't rebel against them and had no moral scruples about anything the *angkar loeu* ordered them to do. Some of the most brutal and vindictive of the *chlops* were teenage boys – young and easily brainwashed into enjoying the power they had over us. We were afraid of them, because whatever the *chlop* reported to the Khmer Rouge was believed without question. If we were accused by the *chlops*, we could be "sent to study" immediately. They became very powerful: they noted every mistake and looked for any excuse to punish or persecute us. As the new-liberated people, we had to be constantly aware of how we behaved. It was a deadly game that we played every day. Make a wrong move and we would be killed.

As soon as we were settled in this new-liberated village, we were divided into groups, each with a leader who controlled and investigated his people and reported anything suspicious to the *angkar loeu*. After four months we were beginning to fear that we wouldn't survive. Even if we weren't denounced by the *chlop*, we would probably die of starvation, because the *angkar loeu* had stopped giving us rice, and our own food had run out. We couldn't get any more: we'd bartered away all the gold, silver, jewellery and other things we'd brought from home to exchange for rice with the people living near our village. Paper money was no use, because the *angkar loeu* had abolished it. At home we used to have plenty to eat, but now we had almost nothing. We'd planted a little garden, but nothing had grown yet. We learned to eat leaves and roots, parts of the banana and papaya trees, bamboo shoots and so on, things which had never appeared on our dinner table.

Some people in our village had already died from hunger and sickness. When they were forced to leave the city, they believed what they were told and took only enough food and clothes for three days. They couldn't cope with living in poverty in the jungle, and their faith in the word of the Khmer soldiers had been rewarded with starvation. Now they didn't dare speak out for fear of being "sent to school", but simply sat and waited for death to come.

It soon became clear that the new-liberated people were not going to survive alone in the jungle. We weren't farmers, and it isn't possible to build a self-sustaining community in only a few months. Having proved our inferiority to the established rural communities, the Khmer Rouge decided that our labour should be put to use. They split up our group and sent us to live and work among the old-liberated people in different villages. When our turn came, my oldest brother and Sophanny were told to go to a different village from the rest of the family. We had never lived apart before, and my father bravely went to see the Khmer Rouge leader to ask permission for Sophoan and his wife to live with us. He came back looking unhappy: the leader had rejected his request and said that under no circumstances would the *angkar loeu* alter its decision. I admired my father's courage, because questioning a leader could be considered an act of serious rebellion.

When it was time to leave we cried and hugged our brother and his wife. In the year since we left the city we'd faced many difficult situations, but now it seemed as though the family would be torn apart. My mother cried and cried.

"I don't want to lose you," she wept. "No matter how hard it's been, we've helped each other. Whatever we have, we share; whatever we eat, we eat together. We want to live together and care for one another, and if we die, we'll die together." But her words couldn't change the situation.

On impulse, Sophoan ran to beg one more time for permission to come with us. When he arrived at their shelter, the leader said,

"What do you think you're doing? Your father's just been here. We didn't approve of that, and now you come to ask for yourself. Go away, or we'll send you to study."

My brother almost choked when the soldier said that, but he didn't give up. Then the soldier noticed that he was wearing an "Orient Three Stars" watch, a popular brand.

"*Mith* (comrade) Sophoan, may I see your watch?" he asked.

My brother handed it over quickly and said, "Do you like it? You can have it."

The man nodded. "You may go with your family," he said.

Sophoan bowed down respectfully and thanked him, then he ran back to us, jumping and waving his hands and yelling, "We can come! We can come with you!"

We put everything we owned onto ox-carts driven by the old-liberated people, and plodded behind them to our new destination. We didn't know what the new place would be like, but at least there would be food to eat and water to drink. It had to be better than this. We left behind the shelter we'd built with our own hands, where we had stayed for almost a year. It wasn't a good place to live, but it was our first jungle home and I kept looking at it until it disappeared from sight.

There is an old Cambodian saying, "There is a road, but no people are walking on it; there is a house, but no people are living in it." Now we saw it for ourselves: the Khmer Rouge had emptied whole cities. Everybody had been forced into the countryside. Inhabited houses became uninhabited. Streets once full of people became deserted: no one walked on them. By the roadsides lay the rusting remains of cars and bicycles, discarded bags and belongings too heavy to carry on the long march into the forests. Paper money, now worthless, blew in the streets with the red dust. The cities were ghost towns. On 17th April 1975 the people were forced into the killing fields, and the Cambodian proverb came true.

CHAPTER TWO

NEW DESTINATION

"We will live and die together as a family. We will never forsake each other." My family's commitment.

The sun had almost set. We had walked about twenty miles to our new destination, Thlok village, which had a population of approximately four hundred people. They were all old-liberated people who had been evacuated by the Khmer Rouge in 1970, and had returned to their village the year before we arrived. They greeted us kindly, shared their lodging with us and even gave us rice.

At first everything seemed to be turning out well. After the first week, we were all assigned to our work places, depending on our physical ability. All the communes were organised along similar lines: my parents and their younger children (including me) shared a house, while the older ones were sent away from home to work with the mobile youth workers' groups. Sophoan and Sophanny had their own home in the village, not far from ours. My mother was assigned to work in the fields with the women's group and my father worked with the older men's or *tata* group. My three younger brothers and little sister stayed at home since they were too young to work.

I was assigned to take care of the cows and water buffaloes with five old-liberated children and two older people in our team. I liked going out into the fields: I could play with the old-liberated children, and I got on with them very well. I became good friends with Phoeun, who was very generous and gentle. When we were working outside we played and went everywhere together.

Each morning I packed rice for my lunch and went out to take care of the cows and water buffaloes. Being out in the fields was a good opportunity to get additional food for my family: the flooded rice paddies were surrounded by low embankments, and in the muddy water within these low walls lived hundreds of frogs, crabs and fish. I thought the other children were lazy because they didn't join me. Perhaps they didn't really care about their families, but I felt a very strong sense of responsibility towards mine. After all, with my older siblings working far away from home, I was now the oldest one left in the family. The others were allowed to come home for only one week every three months, but when they came, my older brothers took me fishing, and I'd become very good at it. I also learned to set up traps to catch hares and rabbits, and sometimes I was successful. Since there was no beef or pork, hare and rabbit meat were the next best thing.

Whenever my brothers came home, they salted and dried the fish they caught, left some for us and took the rest away to supplement the rice they were given when they were working. During their short visits, we all talked together about how life was treating us. Once they confided that they were thinking of running away to Thailand. My parents were afraid for them, and told them not to do anything against the law of the *angkar loeu*. The only thing my brothers feared was that after they escaped, the *angkar loeu* would persecute the rest of us and accuse us of being the *khmang* ("enemy"). We would surely be "sent to school". It wouldn't have been difficult for my brothers to get to Thailand, but they decided not to go because of the possible repercussions for the rest of the family. While we were still living in the new-liberated village in the jungle, we had promised to stay together. We would never betray one another: if we lived we would live together, and if we died, we would die together. It was our family's commitment to each other.

When the rainy season came there were plenty of fish, frogs and crabs around, and the *prothean phoum*, or village leader, allowed us to catch as much as we could. We were fortunate in this village: the leader had been a Buddhist monk when he was young, and he had a compassionate heart which really cared for his people. Although he was serving the Khmer Rouge as a leader, he seemed to have very high moral standards: whenever there was bad news he would come to warn us. He was afraid of the *angkar loeu* too, and reminded us not to rebel against them.

At first, no one had quite been able to believe what was actually happening: the Khmer Rouge propaganda had all been about liberation and peace. But gradually even the most out-of-the-way villages began to have their share of bloodshed. People would be taken away "to study" and never come back; they would be buried in shallow graves, which were washed away by the first rains, so that bones and pieces of cloth would be visible in the earth, and sometimes corpses would be left bloated and rotting in the jungle. No one was supposed to travel without a permit, but eventually word of these things got back, and people lived in fear. Even good men like our leader, who didn't approve of what was going on, knew that if they objected they would be the next ones to be killed, so they kept quiet.

For the first few months we were aware of very little social or political pressure. There were no *chlops* to spy on us, and we got along well with our neighbours. To be worth keeping alive, you had to prove that you were serving the revolution by being productive in the fields: as long as we kept working hard, they liked us.

I had to work long hours, but I was helped by having a good friend to play with as we took care of the cows and the water buffaloes together. Phoeun and I really liked each other, and Phoeun's parents liked me as well. When he had good food at home, he would invite me to eat with them, and sometimes I even stayed overnight at his house.

Then my father was sent away to work for three months, without being told what his job would be. He had a good understanding of the Khmer Rouge mentality, and it led him to fear and distrust any order from the *angkar loeu*. He wasn't sure if he would be allowed to come back to see us, and we were afraid that he was going to be "sent to school". My mother spent a lot of time praying to Buddha to protect him.

It was the first time my father had been away from us since we left the city, and the house felt strangely empty. My mother was pregnant at the time and there was no one except me to care for her. When she fell ill, a couple of months later, I had no idea what was wrong with her. Her work was very hard: the women would be bending over all day, planting rice seedlings in the flooded paddy fields, pressing each plant into the soft mud, often with leeches sticking to their bare arms and legs. Even though she became very weak, she forced herself to carry on working, because she was afraid her group leader would accuse her of being lazy. The villagers thought we pretended to be sick because we didn't want to work. It was true that sometimes our exhaustion was caused not by physical illness but by our psychological state: we were uprooted, powerless, afraid and depressed. As for my mother, she went on working until she was too ill to get up from her bed. Then they gave her permission to stay at home until she was better.

Around this time Sophoan was also sent away to work, leaving his wife Sophanny behind. She came to our house every night to prepare food and look after my mother, and I was grateful because it was comforting for me to have her there. No one could tell us what was wrong with my mother: there was no family doctor in the village, because all the medical professionals had been killed in the purge of intellectuals. Sick people would go to see the *kru khmer*, a kind of shaman, but we never did that because we didn't believe in their practice. I felt helpless and afraid, especially when I saw her praying to Buddha to help her and to bring my father back safely. I had no idea whether he would ever come home: perhaps the *angkar loeu* had already killed him.

When at last my father arrived home, we were overjoyed to see him. The village leader seemed to be happy and relieved too – I couldn't understand why. Surely he was the one who had sent my father away for months. Hadn't he wanted him to be killed by the Khmer Rouge? Had he expected him to come back? There were no answers.

My father saw at once what was wrong with my mother: she had malaria, but of course we had no medicine to treat her. At first it looked as if nothing could be done, but then the leader gave my father permission to take her to the hospital, thirty miles away, and even allowed us to use an ox-cart to drive there.

On the way, my father told us what had been happening to him. He had been sent away as a test: a whole group of new-liberated people (former professors, teachers and other professionals) were sent to destroy a Buddhist temple. If they refused to do so, they would be killed. The Khmer Rouge believed that religion was a waste of time, and anyone who wanted to worship the statues of Buddha was *khmang*, and should be destroyed.

When my father arrived at the temple he had met an old friend, also a teacher, who had been sent on the same mission. He told my father, "Whatever the Khmer Rouge soldiers tell you to do, just do it. Don't rebel against them. They want to test us to see if we still believe in religion. A few people are missing already because they refused to do the work."

My father was horrified: for someone like him, born and raised in a Buddhist home, to smash a statue of Buddha was like killing Buddha himself, and his own soul too. If he did as the soldiers ordered, he would be allowed to live longer. If he refused, he would be killed, and his family would suffer. He had no alternative. Closing his eyes and asking Buddha to forgive him, he joined the others in pounding at the temple wall. Inside his heart, he cried and cried. It was very hard for him, yet he had no other choice: he was being watched closely by the Khmer Rouge soldiers all the time.

One day, while he was working, a soldier asked him what he did before the liberation, and he replied honestly that he had been a teacher. When he told his friend about this conversation, he suggested that my father should try to escape at once. People who told the Khmer Rouge about their true background often went missing during the night. My father was terribly afraid, especially when a group of soldiers passed close by his shelter; he thought they were coming to kill him. The friend suggested that they should both try to escape over the border to Thailand, but my father refused. He wouldn't leave his family behind to suffer alone.

The next day, another soldier asked my father the same question: "What work did you do before you were liberated?" Once again my father told the truth, though with a fearful heart. The soldier replied, "At least you're being honest with the *angkar loeu*. If you'd lied to us, we'd have sent you to school." This was a huge relief, though my father still didn't feel entirely safe. There was no guarantee of a free life these days, and no one could predict the outcome of the evil game the soldiers played with the lives of their captives.

Shortly after this my father was reassigned to work in the kitchens, and his friend went missing. A week later the remains of his body were found in the jungle. He had lied to the soldiers and told them he was a farmer; consequently he was killed and his body left on the ground to be eaten by the wild animals. This incident made my father more fearful than ever. He was very tempted to run to Thailand, but he couldn't bear to leave us behind. He had no way of sending a message home, and we had no way of contacting him, and about a month later he was moved on again. This time he was assigned to cut bamboo in the jungle. Of the two hundred men in his work-party, only one hundred returned. My father was one of the lucky ones.

We were horrified by my father's stories. My mother said little, but she kept weeping silently. She was afraid of going to hospital, and she was worried about everything: her unborn baby, the children she had left at home, and her older children who were working far away.

When we arrived at the hospital, we could see at once that it wasn't going to help. The place was shabby and dirty, with poor sanitation and no qualified staff. Most of the workers were illiterate and knew nothing about medicine. We didn't want to leave my mother there, but we couldn't go back either: if we did, she would surely die.

We had to stay overnight, because the oxen were exhausted, and my parents talked for a long time about what to do. My mother was sure she would die anyway, and she didn't want to die in that hell-hole. She just wanted to be with my father. He thought she should at least stay and rest there. I fell asleep while they were still arguing.

In the morning, my father went to see the woman in charge, who reassured him that my mother would be taken care of. She admitted that the hospital had no medicine at the moment, but she was sure that the *angkar loeu* would supply some soon. In the end my mother agreed to stay for a week; it was the first time I'd ever been parted from her. I gave her a hug and said, "Take good care of yourself, *mak,*" and then we hitched the oxen to the cart and set off for home.

My father and I had never spent much time together. Before the war he used to set off early for work, and return very late, so that I saw him only at dinner, and seldom had a chance to talk to him. I was a troublesome child: one year, I fell down from a tree and broke my right arm, and had to have an operation in hospital. At the time my parents were away on a business trip (my mother ran her own business, buying and selling rice) and my brother had to call them home to take care of me. They lost a lot of money that year because of me. Now at last, even though my father didn't say much about it, I knew he didn't blame me.

Jolting homewards on the ox-cart I felt almost contented. Life was hard for us – far from home and made to work like slaves in a strange place, constantly in fear of our lives, and now leaving my mother in that dreadful hospital – yet I was deeply happy to have this time alone with my father. It felt like a special blessing, and it brought us more closely together. It was a long, slow journey, and we had time and leisure to talk properly for the first time. He asked me about my friends and my work in the fields, and we talked about life, and about what had happened to all of us. I confessed that when he went away I hadn't expected ever to see him again.

When we arrived home, I went to work as usual and my father was sent back to work with the older men. Five days later, when I came home from the fields and hurried into the house, I saw my mother sitting in her usual place: she was back! I ran across the room and threw myself into her arms. I was so happy to see her that I didn't ask how she felt, and I didn't realise at first that she was sicker than ever.

She said that six days in the Khmer Rouge hospital was like being in hell. The story about the medicine had been a lie. She had been placed in a special room with other new-liberated patients, and no one asked what was wrong with her. They gave her some medicine and told her to take two tablets a day, but she didn't take it because she thought it looked like hare's dung. I thought she was joking, but she showed us some and it was true. No matter what diseases the patients had, they were all given the same tablets, and two patients – new-liberated people – died after being injected with water from filthy syringes. The Khmer Rouge had outlawed the use of any Western medicines, and only traditional herbal remedies were allowed. My mother became terrified of the Khmer Rouge doctors. She was sure if she stayed in the hospital she was going to die, and no one would bury her. Finally, she decided to come back and die at home.

Now we were desperate: my father dug up some roots from the jungle and prepared them in the Khmer traditional way to cure her malaria, but it didn't help her because she had been ill for so long already. My mother kept talking about how unfair life was: she didn't deserve this. She had always been a good person. On every Buddhist holy day, she prepared food and took it to the temple to offer to the monks. She helped poor people on the streets. She had given money to build a temple and a school. She would never kill living things. She would never be unkind to people. She always had compassion for the poor. Did she deserve to suffer like this? Was it her karma?

She kept saying how much she longed to see all my brothers and sisters one more time before she died. It hurt me to see my mother like this: I was young, but I understood enough about life and death to know what was happening. When I went out to work I tried especially hard to find food to help her regain her strength. I wanted her to be well and happy as she had been when we lived in the city.

Shortly after her return, all my brothers and sisters were allowed home for a week, and they were shocked by her appearance: her skin was yellow and she was thin and haggard. However, by an amazing chance, one of my brothers had brought some malaria medicine home with him. When he was first sent away to work, he fell ill and went to see a Khmer Rouge nurse. She understood only one kind of medication, which she gave to everyone who consulted her – the hare's dung tablets. My brother found out that she actually had several drugs in storage, but she couldn't read their labels, which were in French, and she didn't know how to use them. She let him select his own medicine, and he identified and helped himself to several drugs which he thought might be useful.

My mother took the new tablets and to our delight she soon began to feel better. Despite everything, we considered ourselves lucky. This was a fortunate place to live: the village leader didn't persecute us, no *chlop* came to investigate us, and we had enough to eat. Although my mother had been through a hard time, she had survived her illness, and about three months later her baby, another boy, was born healthy and normal. We all loved the new baby. My father named him Thlok Phirounn, because he was born in Thlok village. He was born in a hostile environment at the wrong time, and my brothers and sisters who were away from home had yet to see his face, but I knew they would love him when they finally got a chance to see him.

About four months after Thlok was born, the political situation changed again. The old leader was fired because he was too nice to the people, and the new one assigned by the *angkar loeu* was a strict, serious Khmer Rouge soldier in his late twenties. He looked mean and nobody liked him. Suddenly the village was a very quiet place: everyone was scared. Before he left, the old leader told my father about the new one and warned us to take great care. The new man had asked him a few times about how we were behaving: he had been assigned specifically to destroy the *khmang* of the *angkar loeu* in that village, the primary *khmang* being the new-liberated people. We would be his first target. Each night, he was going to send *chlops* to eavesdrop on us. When we heard this, we despaired: if we made just one wrong move, we would be in trouble.

One man in our village was overheard complaining about life under the control of the old-liberated people. A *chlop* took him away in the night. His wife hoped that he would be punished and released, but he never came back. They killed him in the jungle close to the village, and they didn't bury him deep enough: the foxes came and ate his flesh. Everyone learned a lesson about complaining.

Fortunately, not long after this my family and some other new-liberated families were sent off to another village called Kok Preach, the home of about five hundred old-liberated people. Once again we settled in: the old-liberated people helped build a small house for our family, and we were quickly assigned to work teams. My father went to work with the *tata* (older men's) group, my mother went into the fields with the other women, and I worked with the children's mobile team. My brothers and sisters on the youth mobile team were still away and at first they didn't know we'd been moved on, but eventually we were reunited and they were reassigned to the youth mobile team from the new village.

I didn't like our new situation. I worked from five o'clock in the morning to five o'clock in the evening digging irrigation channels in the fields. The soil was heavy and the job was really beyond me, but I was twelve now, no longer a child. If I didn't work, I wouldn't get a food ration. We hardly saw one another and we didn't talk much, because when we came home it was already dark and we were tired out. Everybody had to work, and no grumbling was allowed: complaints would be swiftly punished by the *chlops*.

In this village, the old-liberated people were very unkind. They seemed to be prejudiced against us, even accusing us of being Chinese because our skins were fairer than theirs. I didn't understand why they hated the Chinese so much. I often heard them complaining about us because we had once lived in the city. They hated all professional people because we were not like them, and the doctrine of the communists was that only those who did manual labour were worthwhile. A dark skin suggested that you were a field worker, out in the sun all day, growing rice to support the revolution. A light skin indicated that you were one of the corrupt class of capitalists. All this class hatred and anger had been planted in their hearts by the teaching of the Khmer Rouge.

Three months after we moved there, my sister Sopheap married Chhounly, a friend she had known since her schooldays, and moved away to live with her husband in a different village. The marriage ceremony was a strange one: probably a hundred couples were paired up, more or less randomly, and pronounced husband and wife on the spot by the *angkar loeu*. It seemed that so many people had died, so many communities had been broken up and relationships broken, that life everywhere was in turmoil. People were dispirited and the population was not renewing itself. It had occurred to the *angkar loeu* that the country needed children to farm in the future, so they selected young men and women to be, in effect, breeding stock: to produce children for the revolution. Some couples had never met before that day, but they had to agree to the marriage – if they rebelled, they would be killed. My sister was very lucky because she already knew her fiancé and they were engaged in the traditional manner, but we didn't have a chance to share in her wedding, because only parents were allowed to be present. Many of the couples were given a few days together and then separated again into their male and female work parties: the *angkar loeu* had abolished religion, traditional marriage and family life. Sopheap was allowed to go with her husband to his village, to help look after his mother. We were sad that she was moving away, because it was the first time any member of our family had had to leave us. In fact, her marriage was to save Sopheap's life.

Not long afterwards there was another reorganisation of work duties. My two older brothers left us again; as usual, they were sent to work with a youth mobile team far away from home. It was the last time I ever saw them. However, my older sister Sopheavy was allowed to stay at home with us and work in the village. I was pleased, too, when I was reassigned to take care of the cows and water buffaloes with the old-liberated children. It was much lighter work than digging, and I didn't have to listen to any more hateful comments from the people in the village about being a "Chinese" boy.

CHAPTER THREE

A STRANGER

"Do not forget to entertain strangers, for by so doing some people have entertained angels without knowing it." (Hebrews 13:2)

I was back at my old work, taking care of the cows and water buffaloes as they grazed. It was a different village, these were different fields, and I missed my good friend Phoeun, but otherwise things were much the same. I enjoyed taking care of the animals, and I saw every day as an opportunity to forage for extra food: if I couldn't catch any frogs or crabs I would pick fruits or edible leaves. Some of the other children, especially the leaders of our group, teased me for thinking about my family all the time, but I ignored them. Most of them played or slept while we were out in the field, but they told me to follow the water buffaloes all the time, and I had to obey them or I would be punished.

It wasn't only children who feared being reported to the leadership and punished: our parents were just as terrified as we were. At night, when we were lying in our beds, I would sometimes hear the low voices of my parents as they talked. If a dog barked outside, their whispers would stop immediately.

You never knew when a *chlop* was lurking by the windows or under the stilts of the houses, listening for anything that could be used to incriminate us. The next thing would be the knock of the soldiers on the door. If you were lucky, you'd be taken to a village meeting and beaten; if not, you'd be taken "to study" in the jungle and never seen again. We were afraid of the *chlops*: they were cruel people who would kick a child just for fun.

It's hard to begin to recount the examples of cruelty that surrounded us every day. We were most afraid of the teenage boys in the village; they were willing to do whatever they were ordered and were determined to serve their evil leaders. One young boy joined the Khmer Rouge soldiers and was quickly brainwashed by his leader. When a *chlop* discovered that his father was having an affair with another woman, the boy was ordered to arrest him. He tortured his own father and accused him of being the *khmang* of the *angkar loeu*. The penalty was execution, so he killed him, apparently without any compunction. How could a boy be programmed for evil so easily?

I heard about another friend of mine who was trying to rejoin his family when he was captured by the Khmer Rouge and forced to join them. His family had been arrested by some of their former servants who had joined the army, and they were sentenced to death. "They're all capitalists," said the servants, "and the country doesn't need capitalists." They ordered my friend to kill his own family. He couldn't do it, and planned to run away, but he was caught and hauled back to be executed with them. The soldiers gave him a choice: if he wanted to live to serve the *angkar*, he had to kill his family; if he refused, he'd be killed too. He refused, but his father loved his son and wanted him to have a chance to live.

"Kill us, son," he said, "and save yourself."

His father kept pleading until he finally agreed, and the Khmer Rouge untied him and gave him a gun. They stood behind him, pointing their guns at him, prepared to shoot him if he tried to turn against them. He closed his eyes and pulled the trigger. Many times. One bullet for each of his family. The Khmer Rouge enjoyed the game and finished it by shooting him, too. Afterwards, they didn't bury the bodies, but left them to be eaten by the dogs.

It was hard to imagine what could have made ordinary men so cruel, but one young soldier arrested after the war explained how they became so violent. His family had been killed when he was about nine years old, and the Khmer Rouge soldiers looked after him. In effect, they became his new family. They told him that General Lon Nol's soldiers had killed his family, and that it was his job to avenge their deaths. From 1975 to 1979 he fearlessly killed more than a hundred people: when he was asked why, he said that the *angkar loeu* had ordered him to do so. If he didn't obey the *angkar loeu's* command, they would kill him. He said he was afraid the first few times: he had to close his eyes to shoot. After a while he became bolder and enjoyed killing his victims, the *khmang* of the *angkar loeu*. At first he shot people from behind, but then he started killing them by clubbing them on the head and neck, by cutting their throats and so on. After the first few dozen, he became addicted to killing and had favourite ways of doing it. Sometimes, before killing the women, he would undress them and use his knife to play with the women's breasts. Here was a human whose soul was poisoned with evil.

I could see that the power of this army was evil, but I knew we had to be humble if we wanted to live in peace. My father always told us, "Speak as little as possible." He wanted us to pretend to be deaf and stupid and never speak a word out of place; he wanted us to bow down and submit to them. Was he teaching us to be weak? I don't think so: rather, he understood their mentality. They wanted instant obedience, and their cruelty was such that they wouldn't think twice about inflicting punishment or even death for the most trivial of offences. They had to prove that we, the new-liberated people, were their inferiors and wholly in their power.

Life under such a system was very frightening. We were constantly afraid of making a wrong move. If we heard noises in the night – distant knocking, shouts, screams, shots – we cowered in our beds. The next day someone – sometimes a whole family – would be missing. We gave no sign that we'd noticed. All we could do was pray that we would survive these terrifying times.

One day when I was going to the fields I met a stranger near the river. He was an elderly man, about sixty-five. I supposed that he was from a different village, perhaps far away, since I'd never seen him before, though it was unusual to see strangers. People weren't allowed to travel around without a permit. He looked skinny and weak, as if he hadn't eaten anything for a long time. I felt sorry for him because of the way he looked, but I didn't speak to him. However, he came up to me and said, "*Chao proh* (grandson), wait a minute." In Cambodia, it is customary for older people to call a child "*chao*" or "*chao proh*".

"I'm very hungry, child. I've had nothing to eat for two months. Will you share your lunch with me?"

My lunch was meagre enough: a little rice and salted fish, wrapped in a banana leaf. If I shared it with him, I'd go hungry for the whole day. But then, not sharing it would be selfish, and my parents had taught me not to be selfish. I couldn't bring myself to say yes right away: I looked at him and then at my lunch, and I knew I couldn't refuse such a gentle request.

"You can have some of it," I said, "but please keep some for me." Then I handed over my food.

I sat down and watched him eat: I could see he was very hungry. Perhaps what he told me was true – perhaps he hadn't eaten for two months. I wondered if anyone could really survive without food for so long. He ate without talking, really enjoying it. When he'd finished half of it, I thought he might give the rest back to me, but he showed no sign of slowing down. In fact, he kept eating faster, as if someone was racing with him. I wanted to tell him to stop eating my lunch, but I knew that it wouldn't be polite. I just looked at him with great regret in my heart, wondering why I'd been so nice to him. It wasn't as if I had much to eat myself. When he'd finished every last bit of my lunch, he thanked me.

"You're a good boy. It's nice of you to give up your lunch for me. You're so kind. I never met a boy like you in my life."

By this time I wasn't interested in his compliments, I was too angry. "If he's so grateful, at least he might have saved a bit for me," I thought. He didn't seem to realise that I was actually very angry with him.

He started asking me questions: "What's your name? Where did you live before the fall of the country?" But I didn't answer them. I sat in silence for a while, then I got up to leave – I had to go to work. When he saw me getting up, he said, "Walk forward about a hundred yards and then come back." I didn't like the way he spoke to me, but I was used to obeying orders, and I was trained to be polite to my elders. I walked forward and then back towards him as he instructed. Then he said, "Sit down again."

"You're going to face a bad situation in the next six months," he said. "Your family are all going to be killed, but you'll survive in the jungle. You won't die, but you will have to endure a lot of pain. You're a special person in your family, and someone has been protecting you since you were born. If you want to know how you were born, you should ask your father."

It made no sense to me at all. I couldn't understand what he was saying, and I didn't like his words about killing. He went on. "When you're in the jungle, a man from your village will save you. Then you'll go back to the city. You will intend to go east, but eastward will not be your destiny. Instead you will go on to the west. You will have a good life, but you won't find it easy. Then when time has passed, you'll come back to this country . . ."

I wasn't interested in listening any more. Nothing he was saying made any sense, and I thought he must be crazy. At first I'd felt sorry for him, but now I was just angry. First he ate all my lunch, and then he told me bad things about my life, as if it was some sort of horrible curse. I turned my back on him and walked away as fast as I could.

It was late evening by the time I went to collect the animals. As I went home, I kept thinking about the stranger. I was very sceptical about his mysterious words, but I couldn't think why he'd make up such horrible things. There was enough real killing and death going on, without trying to frighten a child with threats about the future. I did wonder why he'd talked about when I was born, and I wondered whether to tell my father. In the end I decided to say nothing – the family would almost certainly consider the old man's words a curse. However, my curiosity had been aroused: perhaps one day I'd ask my parents about when I was born.

A few weeks later, my father was allowed to take a break from his work one evening, and he said, "Come *reiy sontouch* (fishing) with me." My father liked taking me on fishing trips because I wasn't afraid of the dark, and I loved going night fishing because it gave me an opportunity to get closer to him.

With my older brothers away I was the oldest son at home, and we had grown closer ever since the long journey back from the hospital.

We arrived at the lake and set up our *sontouch* (fishing lines); it was dark and the mosquitoes were buzzing around, so while we waited for the fish to bite we lit a fire. I sat close to the fire and looked at my father intensely: his face was lit by the flickering flames. "Are you tired?" he asked me, and I said, "Yes, a bit." He turned away to light a cigarette, and I thought, "This is a good moment to talk to him."

"Papa, may I ask you a question?" I asked.

He smiled and nodded.

"Why was I named Sokreaksa?" I asked.

He looked thoughtful for a moment, and then said, "Why do you want to know about your name? None of your brothers and sisters ever wanted to know how we chose their names. You're the only one who's ever asked me that."

"I'm just curious, that's all," I said.

"Well, on the night you were born there were thieves about in Kampongtayong village, though I didn't know that at first. I got up to call the midwife and neighbours to look after your mother. When I came back, it was about two o'clock in the morning and everybody in the house was awake and talking. Five or six thieves were hiding in the bushes outside our house."

I interrupted him. "How did you find out there were thieves about?"

"In those days, security wasn't very good. During the day, the police patrolled the town, but at night thieves came out and skulked around the houses, looking for what they could get. They'd get into houses while people were asleep, but they had guns, and if the people woke up, they sometimes shot and injured them. We wouldn't have known the thieves were there, but you came into the world crying at the top of your voice, and you didn't stop! Everyone could hear you. The people in the next house, and all the other neighbours realised you'd been born, so they came out and walked across to our house to see you. That's when they saw the thieves: they had guns and they were climbing over our fence. All the neighbours shouted and chased after them, and the thieves ran away. After that we took precautions to protect the family and our property. In the morning, your aunts and your mother decided to name you Sokreaksa. 'Sok' means happiness, and 'Reaksa' means to take care of, prevention or protection. 'Sokreaksa' means that the day you were born your crying brought us safety and happiness. That's how you got your name."

I had to believe this strange story, because my father wouldn't have made it up. It made me happy to think that I'd protected my family: it was a good name.

I thought again about the stranger, but I couldn't see any connection with what my father told me. I didn't want to ask my father anything else, because I wasn't ready to tell him about my encounter in the fields. I didn't want to believe what the old man had said. Anyway, I'd always rebelled against superstition and irrational belief: I didn't like crazy people who pretended to know what would happen in the future.

Three months after this, our village ran out of rice. We were living in the middle of one of the richest farming areas in the country, but the *angkar loeu* was organising the distribution of food, and our harvest was taken away and we weren't given sufficient rations for our village. Fortunately, there were still edible leaves and bamboo shoots in the jungle. We ate them just to survive, though we became very much weaker than before: there wasn't much nutrition in leaves, but people who didn't eat them died of starvation.

We were still expected to carry on with our hard physical work. It was gruelling enough for the peasant farmers when our rations were cut, but at least they were used to manual labour. For the new-liberated people from the towns – businessmen, shopkeepers, office workers, teachers – it meant a slow death from starvation and exhaustion. They weren't used to being desperate enough to adapt to anything, and many of them hadn't learned to forage as we had. They grew so weak that they couldn't even carry the bodies of their family and relatives for burial. Some couldn't even stand up.

Starvation was terrible: dying of hunger wasn't an easy death, but staying alive wasn't easy either. We'd faced a lot of difficult times in recent years, but they were nothing like this. A few days before he died one of my friends said to me, "Reaksa, you know I'm going to die very soon. Perhaps today or the day after. I just wish I could have a grain of rice to put into my stomach. Then I could die happily." I couldn't help him: he died a few days later. It was terrible to watch a dear friend starve. It was sadder still to see his emaciated family staggering under the slight weight of his tiny body as they carried him to be buried.

Our family tried to survive in every way we could. We ate terrible things that previously we would never have eaten. We thought of running away from the village, but there were too many of us, and we were all very weak. Even if we escaped from the village we had nowhere to run to. If we were caught, we would be punished even more. Complaining would only give the soldiers an excuse to kill us. It was the fear of death which forced us to keep moving and working, though I was so weak that I couldn't keep up with the water buffaloes – great slow lumbering beasts. By now it was the rainy season and the animals had become difficult to control: they loved to play with water and mud. I didn't have the strength to walk properly, so how could I run after them? I tried to fill my stomach with water and leaves, but it didn't stop my hunger pains. I wished I could live on grass like the cows. Two other new-liberated friends taking care of the animals with me were as ill as I was. We had no physical strength at all, but we went on working because we were afraid of being called lazy and of being killed right away. There was nothing greater than the fear of death, forcing us to work during the day and filling us with despair at night.

Days went by and we endured them. Our only wish was for just a bowl of rice in our stomach; then we could die in peace. Perhaps a stronger wish was that we might die instantly, without having to watch the rest of the family suffering and dying slowly of starvation. We had suffered enough.

My thoughts often turned to the stranger's prediction that my family would be executed in the next six months. I knew it couldn't be true, but I started counting the months anyway. Four months had passed since my strange encounter. The more I thought about it, the less I believed we would be executed: it looked much more likely that we were going to starve to death.

One day I met *mith* Phoeun, the old-liberated boy I used to play with in Thlok village, about five miles away. He was surprised to see me and looked as if he couldn't believe his eyes. The moment we met, he said,

"Reaksa! Are you still alive?"

"No," I responded jokingly, "I'm not alive. You're talking to a ghost."

For a moment he looked really frightened. He thought I really was a ghost! He looked as if he was going to run away, and I had a hard time reassuring him that I was actually alive.

"Phoeun, what's wrong?" I asked. "Why were you so frightened when you saw me?"

He looked around to see if there was anybody nearby, then he motioned me to sit down with him. He shared his lunch with me – I was so happy to get some food – and told me how glad he was to see me alive. At first he didn't want to tell me what had been happening, but finally he took a deep breath.

"Reaksa," he said, "I thought you were already dead, because all the new-liberated people in my village have been 'cleaned' by the new leader. They've all been killed in the last two weeks. I thought you and your family must have been killed too. I've been thinking about you ever since, so when I saw you, I couldn't believe it was you. Do you know that the top leaders of the *angkar loeu* have planned to send all the new-liberated people to school – every one of them? You'll have to run away from your village and hide yourself in the jungle. If I could, I'd take you to live in my house, but I can't. They'd find you. I can't do anything to protect you."

I believed Phoeun absolutely – who would make up something like that? So I said, "Do you know why they're killing them?" He had no idea, but he knew, like me, that most new-liberated people were considered *khmang*. The soldiers told everyone that they supported the Americans – Phoeun said they were believed to be involved with the CIA – and they had to be "cleaned"; otherwise they'd organise rebellions against the *angkar loeu*. I didn't know what he meant about the CIA, and I didn't think he understood it either, but I believed him. I felt as though hundreds of butterflies were in my stomach. With the people in the other village killed, our turn would come soon.

When I arrived home, I told my parents what had happened at Thlok village, but I don't think they took me seriously. It didn't make much difference: even if they had believed me, there was nothing we could do. All they could do was pray to Buddha to save our lives. As far as I was concerned, Buddha was dead, and I hadn't prayed in a long time. But that night, as I watched my parents at prayer, I realised that they felt that our situation had grown suddenly much more dangerous.

Now I began to believe in the stranger. Death was imminent, whether by starvation or execution. All we had to do was wait.

CHAPTER FOUR

TORTURED

"If there is no love, justice cannot exist." My father's words.

A week later, my younger brother Sopheak was arrested by a *chlop* in the village. I looked out of the window to see him being led past with his arms tied behind his back, and I hastily called to my parents. As we came out, the *chlop* hung him on the fence outside the house, and ordered us to stand in line and watch his punishment. I couldn't believe my eyes: how could they punish him any further? He was already so badly beaten up that his face was scarcely recognisable.

We watched helplessly as Sopheak received the worst beating of his life: he was only ten years old. We were powerless to help, unable to protest – to object to what the *chlops* were doing would be rebellion, punishable by death. We could only stand and look at them enjoying their game of torture.

We had no idea what Sopheak was supposed to have done, but we couldn't speak to him. When he began to lose consciousness a *chlop* noticed, and poured water on him to revive him. As I stood watching, I wished God would take my life right then, so I wouldn't have to watch such things ever again.

Where was God in all this suffering? I would rather they tortured me instead of my little brother. My mother stood beside me, beyond tears in her pain: she could do nothing to protect her son. She knew, like me, that to intervene was to be killed.

In a situation of evil such as this, all our normal human responses were crushed. We weren't allowed to express our emotions – it was forbidden to cry out, to weep, even to speak to the poor battered child hanging on the fence. Sopheak was being hurt physically, but we were also being tortured psychologically and emotionally.

What had my little brother done to deserve this? On the ground in front of the fence lay two pieces of corn. Had he stolen it? Even if he had, it wasn't worth such an extreme punishment. He looked so fragile, hanging on that fence: our weeks of starvation had left him thin and weak. I was afraid he was going to die under the beating, but I almost hoped that death would come and release him.

When Sopheak regained consciousness, the *chlop* stood over him.

"Now you must say, 'I will not steal again!'" he shouted. Sopheak could hardly speak because his mouth was swollen and bruised, but he mumbled that he hadn't stolen the corn.

Every time he denied it, the *chlops* beat him again, taking it in turns to hit him. His face was bleeding badly, and they began to kick him in the stomach. There didn't seem to be any part of his tiny body that wasn't beaten, but he was very brave, and he didn't cry or call for help. He just kept saying that he hadn't stolen the corn, but someone had given it to him. The *chlops* were furious that he refused to admit that he was a thief, and they kept kicking him until he lost consciousness again. I couldn't bear to watch, but I had to. I wanted to look away; I wanted to cry out; I wanted Sopheak to die and be spared this suffering; I wanted to kill the evil *chlops* who were doing this to him, yet I felt as though a strange paralysis had set in. I couldn't speak or move, because of my fear. A glance at my parents told me that they felt the same: my mother looked as if she might suffocate, and my father was red-faced, overpowered by speechless anger as he stood there helpless to prevent all this happening to his little son.

The second time my brother lost consciousness, I thought he was dead. His legs had stopped kicking. The *chlop* looked at him and then at us and said, "If any one of you steals like him, you'll be punished like him or we'll send you to school. We want all of you dogs of the Americans to learn a lesson today. You have to be careful. We'll destroy all of you."

Then they started lecturing us about the rule of the *angkar loeu,* and how the way of the Khmer Rouge was better than the old ways. They said, "We don't steal like the dogs of the Americans." They made us stand and listen to them, but we couldn't understand their words: once they'd said that awful phrase, "We'll send you to school", we couldn't hear anything else – it was as though part of us had died already. When they finished their lecture, they said, "Do you understand the law of the *angkar loeu*? You must not steal. If you steal, you will be sent to school to change the American mind." We answered dutifully, "*Bat, mith bong*" ("Yes, comrade").

I didn't believe that my brother had stolen those two pieces of corn: we'd always been taught that stealing was wrong. It was strictly forbidden by our parents. Yet perhaps it was possible – like all of us, Sopheak was very hungry, and we hadn't had any rice to eat for such a long time. Physical survival is a powerful urge: hunger will drive people to steal, cheat or kill. Perhaps he did it because he was hungry. But where could he have got it? No one in this village grew corn. I wanted to ask the *chlops* where my brother was supposed to have found the corn to steal – I wanted to show them how unlikely it was. I wanted them to admit that it was a strange thing that he should find corn in a village where none grew. I wanted justice for my younger brother, but I knew it was a hopeless cause. There would be no justice. My father used to say, "If there is no love, justice can't exist. Don't try to fight for justice when people don't understand the principle of love. They'll never listen to you." He understood the nature of evil; I knew our cry for justice would never be heard.

Once again the *chlops* tried to force a confession from Sopheak: he could no longer open his eyes, but he heard their demands. He shook his head and kept saying, "It was given to me." I was so proud of him. Even in torture he held on to his integrity: he wouldn't deny his own conscience and tell a lie to gain release.

The *chlops* were angry at his refusal, but they'd grown tired of beating him. They unhooked him from the fence and hung the corn around his neck, and then dragged him around the village. They went to the houses of all the new-liberated people, to show them how much they hated thieves, and each time they stopped they hit Sopheak with a stick and forced him to say, "I'll never steal again." Then they told the people that all thieves would be tortured like him.

We were humiliated to see them using my brother as their object lesson, dragging him around the village, but we could not stop them. I feared he would die soon, because his physical condition was very bad. It seemed impossible for him to live much longer. Even if he survived, he would surely be mentally or physically crippled.

While they were dragging him around, we returned to our house, shut the door and wept quietly: we couldn't cry aloud in case anyone heard us. I kept watch near the window, so that if the *chlops* came near, I could signal to my parents. My mother was crying bitterly and praying to Buddha to save my brother, but I couldn't pray. What had my brother done to deserve this? Was it his karma? It just wasn't fair. "Where are you, God? Why are the evil people so powerful? Help my brother, God. Do you hear our cry? Help us!" My father stood silently, holding my mother and trying to console her: it was as though his helplessness had robbed him of the power of speech.

Suddenly I remembered the stranger's words: I knew that everything would happen to me as he had said. Although part of me still struggled with disbelief, I couldn't get rid of the thought. *Mith* Phoeun had told me that all the new-liberated people in his village were already killed. Was it my family's turn? The *chlops* had focused their attention on us. Death was fast becoming a reality. There was no possible way of escape.

An hour after they dragged Sopheak away, two *chlops* passed by our house, carrying the string they had used to bind my brother's hands. They were alone, and I turned to my mother and said, "I think they've killed Sopheak." She cried out, "Oh God, why did they kill my son? God, take my life!" Then she fainted.

My father bent over her: his face was red and his hands were shaking. I knew he felt like me: if he only had the power, he would kill someone; he wanted revenge. But there was nothing he could do.

Suddenly the door burst open and Sophoan, my eldest brother, rushed in. He had seen the *chlops* dragging Sopheak by his house, and he was shocked to see the state he was in. He had no idea that little Sopheak had already been tortured in front of us. Sophoan was stunned to see my mother lying on the floor.

"*Mak, mak,* what's happened to you? Papa, are you all right? What is happening to Sopheak?"

My father only shook his head. I hugged Sophoan and told him what had happened, and we wept together.

"What should we do, papa?" Sophoan asked.

My father said slowly, "There's nothing we can do. If they see us crying like this they'll come to kill us too. They can do whatever they want. We're their prisoners, and our lives are worthless to them. At least if they kill us now, we won't suffer any longer."

My father was right. Some time ago on one of our fishing trips he had said to me, "In a struggle for power there's a winner and a loser. Whoever has a gun is the winner, and the loser becomes a prisoner." If I'd had a gun that day, I would have blown their heads off and become the winner. Since I didn't have a gun, I was the loser. If we tried to get justice for Sopheak, we'd be rebelling against their law. We would die anyway.

Sophoan suggested that I walk around the village to look for Sopheak, to try to find out for sure if he had been killed. We were too afraid to go and ask directly: I was sure that if I did, they would kill me as well. The *chlops* always said, "Whose hair, his head," meaning that each person is responsible for his own misconduct. You were not supposed to take responsibility for someone else's actions.

I was terribly afraid to leave the house, but I had to find out. I walked past more than twenty houses before I saw a group of old-liberated children standing in front of the house of the village leader. Sopheak was in the middle of the group: he had been untied and was standing and holding the two pieces of corn. Two *chlops* were lecturing the children about him.

"Sopheak is the *khmang* of the *angkar loeu*. He stole corn from our people, and the *angkar loeu* hates thieves. You're all faithful children of the *angkar loeu*. You must learn that if you steal, you'll be punished like him. Sopheak is a bad boy, influenced by the Americans. They took our land but we destroyed them all. Now we have to destroy all those who have been influenced by the Americans."

The other *chlop* took his turn. "We arrested Sopheak because he stole corn from our people. If we keep him, we gain nothing. If we destroy him, we lose nothing." When I heard those words, I choked up. I couldn't cry out. Then I saw that one of the *chlops* was holding a hoe. They were going to kill Sopheak! He still couldn't open his eyes because of the blood and the swelling: he couldn't see the hoe, and he didn't even know I was there.

The *chlops* pointed to my brother and asked the children, "Is he the *khmang* of the *angkar loeu*?" The children had learned their lesson well. They answered, "Yes! Kill him! Kill him!" The *chlops* smiled: they had taught the children to hate us, the new-liberated people, people of nothing, useless and worthless.

One of the *chlops* took Sopheak roughly by the arm: they were going to drag him into the jungle. Just then the village leader came out of his door and went over to them. I couldn't hear what he was saying to them, but they stopped what they were doing, and stood together talking a little way off. I edged closer to Sopheak and whispered, "Sopheak, Sopheak, this is Reaksa." He turned his head blindly towards me, but said nothing; he held out the two pieces of corn to me. I didn't dare to go closer or take them from him: I felt as though my heart was breaking.

I tried again. "Sopheak, I love you. I love you so much. Say something to me. I want to hear your last words."

He finally spoke, "I love you, Reaksa." It gave me a warm feeling just to hear his voice. He went on, "As long as you live, remember me. Remember what they did to me. I don't want to live in this world any more. There's too much pain for me.

I can't see you – I can't open my eyes. I know they're going to kill me. I just wish I could see you one more time, Reaksa."

I realised that the *chlops* were looking at us, but Sopheak didn't know that. He went on. "Say goodbye to *mak* and *papa* for me. I love them so much. Tell them I didn't steal this corn. I met your friend Phoeun in the field and he asked me to bring it to you. It's the truth. I didn't steal it."

"I believe you, Sopheak," I said, then added, "stop speaking, they're coming back."

The *chlops* walked towards him and one of them said, "Don't steal again. Take the corn, go home and eat it." Then he kicked him in the mouth, and Sopheak fell to the ground. The other pointed to me and said, "If you steal, you'll be punished like him. Take him home." And they walked away from us. They'd decided not to kill him. He was free!

I ran to him and said, "Sopheak! It's Reaksa! I'm taking you home!" Sopheak rolled sideways and mumbled, "Can you ask them to kill me now, Reaksa? I can't bear it. I can't bear the pain any longer. . . ."

I put my hand to his mouth and said, "Be quiet, Sopheak. I'm taking you home." Weeks of starvation had left me weak, but the love and pity in my heart gave me the strength to lift him in my arms. I carried him through the village, ignoring the curious stares of the people we passed.

At the house, my mother had recovered but she was still crying; when she saw Sopheak, she cried even more. Hugging him, she said, "Oh, Buddha, why did you allow this to happen to us? I've never killed a living thing in my life. Why do I deserve this?"

Sopheak whispered, "*Mak* and *papa*, I love you. Thank you for everything. I want to see your faces one more time before I die, but I can't open my eyes. *Mak*, it hurts – every part of me hurts –"

"Hush, Sopheak," said my mother, "I'm going to clean your face." But Sopheak wouldn't stop speaking: he was sure he was dying. "Papa, where are you?" he said. My father reached out and held him tightly. "Papa, I never stole anything. I told the truth. You taught me not to steal, and I wouldn't do it, no matter how hungry I was."

When my mother had washed him, we could see how badly he was hurt: his eyes were too swollen to open, three of his upper teeth were broken, and his abdomen was badly bruised. I couldn't imagine the pain he was enduring. He kept saying that he wanted to see our faces. We looked at each other: we were sure he wouldn't survive the night. The only medicine we had was a piece of dried black bear bile, which we dissolved in hot water and gave Sopheak to drink. A few hours after he drank it, he said that his body felt very hot inside, and then he slept. Later that night my father woke him and gave him some more.

I tried to sleep, but I couldn't. I was wrestling with anger, bitterness and pain. I was enraged by the injustice: I was angry with God, Buddha, the evil *chlops* and the old-liberated people of the village, who did nothing to stop the torture. I wanted them to pay for what they had done to my brother. My mother didn't sleep either: she prayed all night to Buddha for help. I was afraid that Sopheak would never wake up again, and all night long I listened to his painful breathing.

In the morning I went to look at my brother's body, and to my joy he opened his eyes. He said, "Reaksa, I can hardly move, but I can open my eyes now and see your face. I want to see *mak* and *papa*." He took the bile drink a few more times and gradually he began to improve. He was going to live.

However, although his body began to recover as the days went by, it was clear that Sopheak had been profoundly damaged emotionally by his torture. He couldn't get rid of the horror of what the *chlops* had done to him, and their threats ran endlessly through his mind. He kept telling me that he couldn't live like that, and several times he asked me to cut his throat so that he wouldn't feel the pain any more. I could understand his wish – if I were in his condition, in physical and mental pain, I would want to die, too. But I couldn't do it.

About a week later I met my friend Phoeun in the field, and asked him about the corn he'd given my brother. "Didn't you get it?" he asked. Clearly he had no idea what had happened as a result of his gift. I told him the whole story, and he was horrified.

"Reaksa," he said, "I'm so sorry. I never meant that to happen. I don't know what to do to help. I wish I could take you to live with my family, but I can't. I'm so afraid that I won't see you again. I'd like you to run away, but I know there's nowhere to run to. My parents always ask me about you. They'd like you to come to stay with us for a night, but that wouldn't be allowed."

I knew that Phoeun loved me: he had a compassionate heart, but there was nothing he could do to help me. We sat and talked for hours. He shared his lunch with me, but I couldn't accept his gift of some sweet potatoes that he'd brought for me: I was afraid of being accused of stealing, like Sopheak.

Sopheak was still suffering. Sometimes he muttered to himself, saying, "I didn't steal, it was given . . . I don't know . . . Stop beating me, I know nothing." I thought my brother was going mad – now I know better, and realise that he was suffering from the effects of his traumatic experience. I was often afraid that a *chlop* would hear him, and the punishment would start all over again.

After this life began to improve a little: we had been living on leaves and fish, but the rice was harvested and we were given some to make porridge for our family. The first time we ate rice after all those months of hunger we felt reborn. We began to smile a little. Perhaps we wouldn't die of starvation after all.

During the months of starvation Sophanny had been pregnant; no one knew how she had managed to survive on the little she got to eat, but she did, and gave birth to a healthy boy. Sophoan was so proud of him: the baby looked just like his father. My mother was delighted with her first grandson, and always found the time and energy to visit him, even after a hard day's work. We had added a new member to the family, and we all felt the joy of new life.

Then Sophoan was assigned to work outside the village. We knew he would only be gone for three days, because each man was given three days' ration of rice to take with him. Before he left, he asked me to help his wife by carrying water for her. Then he said, "Reaksa, if I don't come back, tell Sophanny I love her. You must take care of her and my son. They mean so much to me."

I told my mother about our conversation, and she prayed for him every night: we were relieved when he came back safely after the three days. That night there was a meeting for the whole village, and one of the *chlops* stood up and spoke.

"We don't like to have the *khmang* of the *angkar loeu* living among us. We have to destroy them. We need to separate them and us clearly. Do you know the *khmang* among us? He is *mith* Sophoan."

Two of the *chlops* came forward at once and arrested my brother: my heart was in my mouth as they challenged him to confess his crime.

"What do I have to confess?" he asked.

One of the two old-liberated people who were sent to work outside the village with him stood up and said, "*Mith*

Sophoan, you stole our rice! We saw you with it! You're a thief!"

One *chlop* punched Sophoan's stomach and the other one hit him from behind, and he fell down immediately.

A woman in the crowd was saying, "Destroy him! Destroy him! He is the *khmang* of the *angkar loeu* . . ." I didn't know why she seemed to hate him so much but I could see that she was shaking with anger.

Sophoan refused to confess, so he was brutally beaten up. Then a *chlop* grabbed a handful of his hair and yanked his head back. "We'll give you two more minutes," he snarled. "If you don't confess, we'll kill you tonight."

My oldest brother had learned a bitter lesson from Sopheak's experience: he muttered, "All right, I confess. I stole it."

One of the *chlops* said, "He's confessed. He's a thief. What shall we do with him?"

The woman who had spoken before stood up and said, "Kill him! Don't keep him! He is the *khmang* of the *angkar loeu.*"

Once again I wished I had a gun. With a boy's helpless anger, I wanted to blow off her head. But I couldn't do anything. Like my parents, I could only wait to see how they would torture Sophoan. Once again, neither God nor Buddha could help us. There was no justice in our world.

Then the *chlops* said, "Tonight the *khmang* will be punished. We will tie his hands and allow mosquitoes to bite him the whole night. No one is to untie him, or we will kill him and all his family."

Everybody went home except me. I hid in the shadows until everyone had gone, then I crept close to the post of the meeting shelter where my brother was tied up. I whispered, "*Bong* (brother) Sophoan, it's Reaksa."

He whispered back, "Reaksa, go and tell Sophanny what's happening. Tell her I love her and our baby son. Tell her not to worry about me. And tell *papa* and *mak* that I didn't steal the rice, but I had to confess, or I would have been tortured like Sopheak. If they kill me, you must take care of Sophanny and the baby. Remember, when our brothers come home, I want them to name the baby . . ."

I couldn't listen any more. "Enough, *bong*. It's more than I can bear." Tears were pouring down my face as I hugged him and walked away. I went to his house and spoke to Sophanny as he had asked, taking her inside the house so that no one would hear her crying. Then I went home. I knew Sophanny wouldn't be able to sleep that night, and neither could I. I told my father what Sophoan had said, and lay down on my bed, worrying about my brother and his wife.

At about two o'clock in the morning, I gave up trying to sleep. I sneaked out of the house to see Sophoan again, even though I knew it was a stupid thing to do, and it might get me killed. When I reached the shelter I couldn't see him, and at first I thought that they'd already killed him. But as I turned away in misery and grief, I heard a sound in the darkness. It was Sophoan, tethered to another post some way away, and squirming as the mosquitoes bit his bare skin. One of the *chlops* had moved him and taken away his shirt.

I called to him softly, "*Bong* Sophoan, are you okay? I'm coming to untie you." He was horrified. "Reaksa? What are you doing here? Go home at once! You know what'll happen if they find you here!" I went to speak to him, but I heard another noise: someone was coming. I shrank back into the shadows of the shelter, then did as I was told and went home quickly.

My mother was sitting crying on my bed when I got home. She hugged me and said, "This is a dangerous game you're playing. When I heard the dogs barking I thought they'd already killed you. Why can't you do as you're told? What if I lose you even before your oldest brother is gone? Don't you remember in the meeting, they said that if anyone came to untie him, they would kill the whole family . . ."

I knew she was right. If I were caught, I would only be the first one in our family to be killed by the *chlops*: the others would all be killed soon after. I lay down on my bed but my mind was in turmoil. Our family had always been close, and now it was in pieces. Two brothers sent away to work, and who knew if we would ever see them again? Sopheap had gone to live with her husband, and no one had heard from them for months. Sopheak had been tortured, and I didn't know if he would ever recover. Sophoan was tied up in the darkness and perhaps they would kill him tomorrow. There was little future for my nephew and his mother if the *chlops* killed my brother. What was happening to our family? I began to despair. The more I thought about life under the evil power of the Khmer Rouge, the more I realised that we had nothing to live for. Why did we even want to live when we were not allowed to live in peace? All the new-liberated people in the Thlok village had already been killed. When were they coming for us?

The next morning, to our surprise, Sophoan came to our house: they had untied him and set him free. He was weeping with relief and joy, despite the pain in his arms, which were badly swollen because they had been tied so tightly behind him.

He told my father that he had stolen nothing. While he was away working, he saved some of his rice ration each day, so that he could take it home to his wife; when the *chlops* checked his bag they found the extra rice, and accused him of stealing it. "We have to be more careful," said my father.

"They're trying to catch us making even the smallest mistake. We're being watched every day."

We never knew when it would be our turn: there was nothing we could do but wait. There was nowhere to escape to: in a jail without walls, we were the victims of an evil that had no boundaries.

CHAPTER FIVE

EXECUTION

"If we keep you we gain nothing, but if we kill you we lose nothing." Khmer Rouge slogan.

A few days after Sophoan was released, he was sent to work in the fields some distance away, with people from different villages. He wasn't told how long he would be away, but he was issued with an ox-cart and enough rice for at least a month. The night before he left, he asked me again to help Sophanny carry water from the pond. He was concerned about his new assignment: it was unusual for one man to be singled out to go and work away from home. The workers he would be joining spoke Kouy, a different dialect of the Khmer tribal language, and they had a reputation for killing new-liberated people. His final words to me were, "Take care of my son for me if I don't come back." He drove away in the ox-cart: it was the last time I ever saw him.

For the rest of us, life seemed to be getting better: we had plenty to eat, and we were all given a supply of rice that would last at least a year. My mother and my older sister Sopheavy were assigned to reap the rice in the fields, which meant a long walk to work each day; my father was working with other older men close to the village. I was reassigned to the children's mobile team in the village, so I didn't need to go out with the animals day after day. I had time to take care of my younger brothers and sister, and also to catch fish in the river and the lake nearby.

One evening I finished work early and decided to take Sokmeth, one of my younger brothers, fishing. We set up our *sontouch* in the lake and went home, planning to pick up the fish in the morning. That night I had a dream: I saw the stranger I had met six months earlier. It seemed to me that he knew how angry I had been with him: even in my dream I felt the anger again. He was trying to say something to me, but I couldn't understand what it was.

Early the next morning we went out to collect the fish: Sokmeth was happy because we would eat so well that night, but he could tell that I was preoccupied.

"Why are you upset today?" he asked.

I felt very odd, and the image of the stranger filled my thoughts. I couldn't stop the words coming out: "I'm afraid we won't be eating the fish today. I'm afraid we'll all be killed when we get home." Sokmeth gave me a strange look and hurried on ahead. He thought I was being stupid.

When we got home my father was still there, but my mother and Sopheavy had already left for the fields. I went to get water from the pond for my sister-in-law, and that was when I saw the *chlops* gathering in a group, sharpening knives, axes and hoes. I knew something dreadful was about to happen to us and a thousand butterflies started up in my stomach.

I was dressing the baby when a *chlop* came up to the house. He beckoned to my father and said, "*Mith bong* (comrade brother), *angkar loeu* invites you to meet in the shelter now."

My father replied, "I will be there in a few minutes. I need to get dressed first." Then he came to me. "Reaksa," he said, "if they kill me today, I want you and your brothers to kill these people for me." Then he left the house. I trailed behind him to see what would happen.

As soon as he reached the shelter, a *chlop* arrested my father and bound his arms behind his back. One kicked him in the stomach and said, "You are the *khmang* of the *angkar loeu*. You served the American soldiers. You betrayed the country. We will destroy you today."

Then I knew that the day had finally come. Today we would all be killed. I ran home and told the children that our father had been arrested, but I didn't know what to do. My hands and legs were shaking uncontrollably, I couldn't stand and I couldn't sit still, though I felt as if all the strength had drained from my limbs. I hugged my brothers and sister, and they started to tremble like me too. I never knew that the fear of death was so terrible: the children's faces were yellow with fear. Only Sopheak seemed calm. He was sad, but he seemed to have no fear of dying.

Then the *chlops* dragged my father to the house and they called to us to come out. They bound my hands behind my back, but then realised that there was no one to carry little Thlok, so they untied me again. Then they told us, "We will send you to school, because you are the *khmang* of the *angkar loeu*. Go with your father now!" They put the six of us in an ox-cart and drove us out of the village, dragging my father on foot.

About three miles from the village a *chlop* came out of the jungle and told us to stop. He said they hadn't finished digging the grave yet. I looked ahead and saw a group of other new-liberated children with their fathers, but none of the mothers were there – all the women had left early to go out to their work in the fields. I knew the other children – we worked together in the children's teams. I could tell they were frightened like me. I held on to my youngest brother but my arms wouldn't stop trembling.

Even then, there was anger in me, and helpless rage. I wanted to hit the *chlop* driving the ox-cart from behind, but I didn't have anything to hit him with. Besides, what would I do with my brother then? If I hit the *chlop* I wouldn't be able to kill him, though I might hurt him, and the other *chlops* would only carry on with what they wanted to do. I was as helpless as the baby on my lap. I could only wait patiently to be executed.

I got off the cart and carried my youngest brother to my father, who knelt to kiss him and the rest of us. I hugged him but he couldn't hug me back because his arms were bound. He couldn't speak for the tears that poured down his face. I said, "Papa, I would like to thank you so much for being my father." I couldn't say any more: my tears were choking my voice. Then I heard him say, "Reaksa, my heart is torn in pieces. I've lived my life, but you children are too young to die. The baby doesn't understand – he's still smiling. Do the others know we're going to be killed?"

"Yes, I told them after I saw the *chlop* arrest you in the meeting shelter."

My youngest sister Somaly cried, "Papa, I want to see *mak*, I want to hug her and kiss her and say goodbye to her. Where is she?" No one knew the answer. I put my arm round her, and said, "*Mak* will come soon." My little sister was trembling, and she buried her face in my shoulder. She whispered, "I don't want to be born like this again. I want to be born in another country where I won't ever see hunger and killing again." What could I say to her?

Five *chlops* were looking at us and laughing, and I wished that I had a gun to kill them with. Anger welled up in me, but when I turned to look at Sopheak I saw that he wasn't shaking: he looked quite calm and resigned. I think he would almost welcome death: he had tasted it already, and he knew that it meant the end of fear and pain.

My father turned to a *chlop* and asked, "*Mith*, can I have a cigarette before I die?" The *chlop* took a pack of cigarettes from his pocket and offered one to my father; I took it and put it into his mouth, and lit it for him.

As I did it, I thought again about the stranger. What was it he'd been trying to tell me? The only thing I remembered was that I wouldn't die. How could I survive an execution? Yet somehow I was convinced that what he had said was true: I wouldn't die.

After my father finished his cigarette, he asked for one more. The *chlop* gave him one, but it dropped from his mouth. The *chlop* picked it up, stuffed it into his mouth, kicked my father's stomach and then said, "We gain nothing if we keep you, so we're going to kill you now. You're worth nothing to us."

I wondered why they were taking so long to dig the grave, and wished they would hurry up. If I was going to be killed, I wanted to get it over with. My father knelt with us and said, "I want to tell you something." What he said next was like a poem he had just composed in his mind.

"There is a wind of change for sure, but we can't live until the wind of change arrives. One day it will come, but it will be too late for us. I'm sorry I can't be with you to the end, but I want you to know I love all of you. We came together and we'll go together. We lived and we'll die together. We are a family . . ."

He had scarcely finished speaking when the *chlops* came and pushed us forward towards the killing place: it was an old well which had been enlarged to make a mass grave. I choked out, "Goodbye, papa! I love you." He nodded to me, then he called back, "It's time for us to die. I love all of you!" My younger sister began to scream. "Papa, please help me! I'm scared, papa!" My father didn't answer: he was a helpless man about to be killed. I reached out and held her tightly against my side.

My father was standing and facing the grave. They kicked his legs from behind so he fell onto his knees; as he turned his head to look at me I saw them club him with a hoe. He fell forward into the grave with a scream. I was screaming too, a pointless, futile scream: "Help us, God, help us."

Then one of the *chlops* jumped into the grave and turned him over to finish him. I didn't want to watch, but I couldn't turn away: I saw what they did to my father. What I saw filled me with such helpless rage, I thought I would suffocate and die before they hit me.

Then they killed Professor Klok Sarin in the same way. Professor So Soeun screamed loudly and tried to run away: he got about ten yards before three *chlops* tripped him up and axed his head about five times. His children were screaming "Papa! Papa!" as they looked on. After a while his legs and arms stopped moving, and two *chlops* grabbed his legs and threw him into the grave.

Then it was our turn. They made us kneel in front of the grave, and as I knelt I felt a blow on my neck and I fell into the grave on top of my father. He was still alive, and I heard his last few breaths. Then there was nothing. My younger brothers and sister and the other children tumbled into the grave too, on top of me. Finally, they clubbed my baby brother. The first three times they clubbed him he screamed loudly, then they clubbed him one more time and I didn't hear him again. I was still conscious but I couldn't move. I knew that the other children were not yet dead, for the *chlops* jumped into the grave to finish everybody off. There was a sound of hacking blades, and I felt their warm wet blood pour over my body. Some of the *chlops* were cheering on in victory.

When they'd finished butchering, slashing and axing, they climbed out of the grave. I heard one of them say, "I think that one's not dead yet." One *chlop* jumped down into the grave again and pulled a body off me, and hit me with the hoe one more time. It was a heavy blow, but not hard enough to end my life. I knew enough then to lie still. If I'd moved at all, they would have finished me off. Someone began to throw earth on top of us, but then I heard a voice say, "Don't bury them yet: we've still got some more *khmangs* to be destroyed." They left the grave open and went off to find other victims.

I had only one sensation then: the taste of death. Blood flowed out through my nose and mouth and choked me, and I was covered with the blood of my family and friends. I wanted to escape, but I knew I mustn't move a muscle until all the *chlops* had gone. Face down on my father's body, pain and panic took hold of me: I had to force myself to calm down. They weren't going to bury us immediately, and once the killers were out of sight I could get away. I couldn't see what was happening, so I listened: there were no more voices, either from the living or the dead. I waited five minutes after everything was quiet, and then cautiously started to move. I tried to disentangle myself from the dead bodies: it took me almost half an hour to climb out from under their heavy weight, because I was so weak. I crawled out onto the dusty ground and turned around to look at the grave. Everyone was lying dead; some of their throats had been slashed. My three younger brothers' brains had spilled out. My baby brother's head had been clubbed until it was pulpy and one of his eyes was hanging out. As for my father, his throat was slashed and his ribs were sticking out. His eyes were open as though he was looking at me. Slowly I climbed back into the grave, reached down and gently closed his eyes.

I checked everybody in the family, in the faint hope that someone had been left alive like me, but no one had. Then I lay down in the grave again with them, and cried until I lost consciousness. When I awakened, I wondered why I had kept so still when the *chlops* were finishing their killing. If they'd known I was alive, they would have killed me then. Now I had to wait for them to come back and execute me all over again. My father said we would live together and die together. Now my whole family was dead, and I felt as if my head was exploding with grief and emptiness. Young though I was, at that moment I realised that my life was meaningless. I felt as though I was swimming in the sea without sight of land. My only desire was to let them kill me. The pain was too much to bear and I didn't want to live with it for the rest of my life.

I waited there for about an hour, but nobody came. I climbed out of the grave again and looked down at my family lying dead in a pool of blood. As I gazed at them, I realised I could hear birdsong: a small bird was singing happily in a branch above my head. The song infuriated me, and I picked up a piece of wood and threw it. The bird flew off, then came back and sang me its song again. I chased it away again, but once more it returned. The third time it came back, I couldn't chase it off again. Did the bird want me to leave this killing place?

I remembered what the stranger had said – that my family would be killed in six months. His words had come true, though I could hardly believe it. And he had said that I would not die, but I would suffer great pain. That also had come true. What else had he said? I hadn't listened properly, because it had all seemed like nonsense. It was something about the rest of my life. I still didn't know if I would truly live – I had been injured by the blows of the execution – but I decided to leave the grave. I kissed my father and said goodbye to him, my brothers and sister, and to all those lying dead in the grave.

I decided to follow the singing bird eastward into the jungle. I had only walked a few yards into the undergrowth when I saw *chlops* appearing from the west and south, dragging other people towards the open grave. If I had waited for a few more minutes, the *chlops* would have captured me once again. Quickly I looked for a place to hide: I wanted to see who else would be killed today. Suddenly, I saw my beloved mother and my older sister Sopheavy stumbling towards the grave. Their faces were covered with a *krama*, the scarves they always wore, and they were crying bitterly. I wanted to call to my mother, to get her to turn around so I could see her face one more time. I opened my mouth but no sound came out: it was as though I was paralysed. Some power came over me and shut off my voice.

They clubbed my mother and sister, and I watched them fall into the grave. All I wished at that moment was to tell my mother how much I loved her. I wished we had been able to say goodbye. At the same time, my heart burned with rage and I wished I could kill these heartless murderers and put them in the grave they had dug for others. I wished with all my heart that I could save my mother and sister but I was powerless and helpless. I couldn't even scream.

After they had killed almost everyone, a *chlop* hit a beautiful girl and she fell on the ground. I knew she wasn't dead, because I could see her moving. He undressed her and used his stick to play with her nipples and her private areas, while the others laughed and cheered him on. I couldn't understand why they saw it as a game, but I did understand that evil had no boundaries. They played with her and finally they killed her. They grabbed her legs and threw her into the grave, then they took their spades, filled it in with earth and went away.

I sat frozen to the spot. It was over, but I couldn't move or think what to do next. As I sat there, another strange thing happened: I looked down and saw, right beside me, a poisonous snake. I knew the kind of snake it was: if it bit someone, they would die very quickly. Why hadn't it bitten me? Was it time for me to die or not? I spoke quietly to the snake. I said, "Please go away. But if my life is supposed to end today, then bite me and make an end of me." I could hardly believe it when the snake slithered away. I wasn't bitten.

After the *chlops* had gone away I lay down on the grass in terrible pain, filled with questions. Why didn't I die right away? Was there any reason for me to live? First the *chlops* and then the snake – why couldn't I die today?

When the sun had almost set I crept out to the grave. I pounded on it with my hands and hit it with my head. "*Mak,* please take me with you, take me with you. I don't want to live." I called to my mother but she couldn't hear me. I screamed and cried and lamented but no one answered. In that jungle, there was no one left alive to hear.

Finally I bowed before the grave and made three promises to my family. "Mother, father, brothers and sisters, as long as I live, I will try to avenge your deaths. If I fail in this, then I promise that I'll become a monk. If I can't fulfil these two promises, then I won't live in Cambodia any more."

The one thing I wanted above all was revenge, but I knew I was still only a child. How could I ever have the strength to kill the *chlops*? I knew that promise might be impossible. But perhaps, one day, if religion was ever allowed again, I could become a monk. It was an ancient custom that sons should enter a Buddhist monastery for a season, to gain merit for their parents' afterlife. I could serve my parents by doing this, at least. But perhaps that would prove impossible, too. If the Khmer Rouge succeeded in destroying all the Buddhist monasteries, and I failed in this, too, then I would run away – to Thailand, perhaps, or even further. I would leave behind everything I had known, just as the whole of my childhood had just been taken away from me. There would never be any good memories for me here.

After I had made these promises, I sat down and cried until thirst and hunger overcame me. I hadn't had anything to eat or drink since Sokmeth and I returned from fishing in the early morning. Now it was getting dark. I'd never been alone in the jungle before, and I was afraid. I knew that wild animals would be drawn to the grave by the smell of fresh blood, so I couldn't sleep nearby. So I knelt by the grave and said, "Spirits of the thirty-three innocent victims, please protect me tonight from wild animals. I will remember all of you and as long as I live I will pay my respects and show my gratitude to all of you." I made a final bow and left the grave.

About half a mile away I climbed a tree to try to get some rest, but it was full of red ants, so I climbed down again. By this time I was desperate with thirst, and I could think of only one thing to do. I picked up a big leaf, folded it, urinated on it and then drank from it. It tasted terrible, but I couldn't see any other source of water.

Up another tree I found a branch to rest on, but my first night in the jungle was uncomfortable. I was tired and weak, but I had to keep moving all the time because I was being bitten by mosquitoes. My neck was badly swollen, and I couldn't breathe properly; I felt as though something was blocked in my chest. Every time I moved pain shot through my bruised body. I gazed into the inky darkness and wished the sun would rise and end the despair of the night, but I knew the day would bring nothing better. I thought about jumping out of the tree so that I could die in peace and not suffer. But what if the fall didn't kill me? Then I'd be suffering even more. I ended up hugging the tree trunk the whole night through.

I wondered about my older brothers who were working away from home. Had they been rounded up and killed too? Did they know what had happened to us? What about my older sister Sopheap and her husband Chhounly? Were they still alive? I doubted if the Khmer Rouge would let the rest of the family live. They believed that if you want to get rid of grass, you need to dig out all the roots – otherwise it just grows again. If you don't kill the whole family, the survivors will take revenge one day.

The night seemed as though it would never end, but at last the dim dawn light began to grow. My first priority was finding water to drink: I climbed down and tried to lick the dew on the grass. I couldn't do it, so I took my shirt off and spread it on the grass to absorb the dew. When I wrung out the shirt, water came out. At first it tasted terrible because of the blood which had soaked into the cloth, blood that had come from the victims piled on top of me. I tried again and again until I judged that I could drink the water. Then I made a makeshift container from a few big leaves to keep water in. The dew didn't taste good, but it was better than urine. I'd learned my first survival skill in the jungle.

With my thirst satisfied, I went back to the grave. I was surprised when I got there to see how clean it looked. The evening before, blood had covered the ground, but when I came back in the morning, there was nothing. Wild animals had licked up all the blood. I knelt for hours to pay my respects to the innocent victims, until hunger drove me away. I found some bad-tasting bamboo shoots for my lunch, then I returned to the grave. I had nowhere else to go.

I sat there and cried until the sun had almost set; then I left to find a tree to climb for the night. I was afraid to sleep in case I fell, and I went on thinking about my situation. Life alone in the jungle seemed impossible: there was no food or water and my back was very painful. I had a hard time drawing breath. Yet I knew I couldn't return to the village or the *chlops* would kill me. If I escaped to other villages, I might still be killed. In the jungle I was free, yet the place was like a jail without walls. I had no idea of what to do.

In the morning, I climbed down to get water in the same way as the day before, and I tried to store some for the afternoon and evening. Then I went back to the grave: wild animals had dug a hole to try to reach the bodies, so I filled it in and went to search for food. I went further into the jungle than I had the day before, and eventually I found some wild fruit. I wasn't sure if it was edible, but I saw birds and ants eating it so I tried some too. It tasted very good and I picked some for the rest of the day.

I got lost on my way back to the grave, and when I finally found it, the sun had almost set. I didn't stay long, but went and found another tree to spend my third night alone under the thick dark canopy of the jungle. This time I was so tired that I did fall asleep, but I had a terrible dream in which the *chlops* were chasing me. I dreamed that I was running away, and only woke when I fell out of the tree. I wasn't badly hurt, but I started coughing, and every time I coughed I felt a deep pain in my chest, and blood came out of my mouth and nose. I realised that I wouldn't live much longer if I stayed here in the jungle.

In the morning, I came down and drank the dew-water squeezed from my shirt. My fall from the tree made me realise I could hide no longer. I didn't want to bear the pain any more, and I decided to go to the village to ask the *chlops* to kill me and end my suffering.

For the last time I went back to the grave. This time two holes had been dug and flesh had been pulled out: it smelled very bad. A few pieces of cloth were strewn around as well. I tried to fill in the holes with my hands and I knelt there again for a while, grieving and crying. Once again I asked the spirits of the victims to protect me, even though I'd decided to go back to the village to be killed. Then I made three bows and turned my back for the last time on the grave where my family was killed and buried. I left my heart behind with them.

CHAPTER SIX

LIVING AGAIN

"A bad person has good friends and a good person has many enemies." My father's words.

I left my family's grave and set off out of the jungle and into the fields. I was walking with difficulty because of my injuries, but after about three miles I came to a small watermelon farm where two elderly *tatas* worked. I was tired and aching by this time, and I sat down at the edge of the field: I could see the two old men sitting outside their open-sided wooden shelter. I hesitated to go closer: I wasn't sure if they would recognise me, but I knew them, because they came from our village.

By about four o'clock, I realised that the working day was over and the *tatas* would soon be setting off for home. If I didn't speak to them now, I would lose my chance until the morning. I got painfully to my feet and walked slowly towards them. When they noticed me crossing the field towards them they were very surprised: it was unusual to see anyone walking in the fields.

"*Chao*, (grandchild)," one of them said, "where are you from?"

I could tell they hadn't recognised me, so I pointed eastward. "I came from the village there. Could I have some water to drink?"

One man fetched me a cupful of clean water – it tasted wonderful after the dew-water I had been drinking from my shirt. As I drank it, he said, "You must be lost."

"No," I replied. "I was just passing by, and as I was thirsty I thought to ask you for water."

I sat down with them for a while, puzzling about how much to tell them. The truth was, I didn't know if they would take me back to be killed if they knew who I was, and I didn't really know if that was what I wanted. At some moments, when I thought about my family, I just wanted to be killed like them; at other times, sitting here with my sore body at rest and my thirst slaked at last – well, I just didn't know any more. I was worn out with thinking about it.

At last I said, "*Tatas*, I heard that all the new-liberated people in your village were killed three days ago." They looked alarmed, and one of them said, "You shouldn't talk about it. If anyone heard that we'd told someone from outside the village, they'd kill us, too. You've had your drink. Go home to your village before sunset, and we'll go home to ours."

I took a deep breath. "*Tatas*," I said, "I don't really come from over there. I come from your village. I know your names: you are *Ta* Bin and you are *Ta* Chheng." I told them their children's names too, and then my own. I said that I belonged among those who were killed three days earlier.

"Nonsense!" one of them said. "What a pack of lies. Now get yourself home; we're not wasting our time with you."

"I will go," I said. "But let me finish telling you what happened." As I told them how I'd survived for three days in the jungle, their eyes grew wide. I thought they were beginning to believe me, but then *Ta* Bin began to mutter the words of a spell. I knew what it was: a spell to make ghosts disappear! They believed my story of the executions, but they thought I was a ghost from the spirit world!

I could see they were genuinely frightened: they both believed in spirits, and thought that I had come back from the dead. They began to back away from me, and I knew that any minute now they would run off.

"Look at me," I said. "Touch my hand. I really am alive."

Ta Chheng took my hand and said, "He's not a ghost. He really is Reaksa." Then he asked, "How did you get out of the grave? Did they kill everyone else?" I told them my story, but they found it hard to believe. When I'd finished, they told me not to go back to the village.

"They'll kill you for sure if you show your face there again. Run away as fast as you can."

"There's no point," I answered. "I've got nowhere to go, and I'm too tired to run. Tell the village people I'm here. I don't care if the *chlops* kill me, I just want a little rice to eat before I die. I won't be far away. They can come and find me."

I turned and limped away, and when I looked back, they were still staring after me. They watched me until I disappeared into the jungle.

At the edge of the undergrowth I started looking for somewhere to sleep – I wanted to sleep on the ground, but I needed a spot where there were no wild animals. By the edge of the farm was a place that everyone avoided: there were stories about an evil spirit that lived in a tree nearby. Sometimes the spirit looked like a ball of fire in the tree: if anyone saw it, he would get ill and die. I thought the bad spirit might keep the animals away.

I lay down under the tree, and before I slept, I asked permission of the spirit to sleep there. I fell asleep easily, but I was troubled by strange dreams. First I saw a beautiful girl with huge eyes; in my dream I knew she wasn't human, but a manifestation of the evil spirit, but she said nothing to me. When she disappeared I saw a tiger, a lion, and then a big snake. Whenever I opened my eyes there was nothing to see but the darkness of the jungle, but every time I closed my eyes I saw them again. My father always used to tell me to conquer my fears, because if I ever saw anything from the spirit world, the fear alone could kill me. As I fought down my fear, I seemed to see a big ball of fire flying away from the tree towards the east. From that moment on I slept peacefully. It was my fourth night alone in the jungle.

The next morning I went back to the watermelon farm and sat down to wait under a large bamboo that grew beside the path. I waited for a long time, and at last I saw the four *chlops* who had killed my family walking along the path: they were carrying an axe, a hoe, and a big knife. I knew that they were coming to kill me, but I was too exhausted by pain and grief to feel fear any more. I sat still and said nothing. They stood in a group close to the bamboo, but they didn't seem to see me. One of them looked right at me, but his glance swept past, and they carried on walking down the path, still looking around for me. I wanted to call out to them to come back and finish me off, but I felt paralysed, as though something heavy was pressing on me: I couldn't speak or move.

About five minutes passed and the sound of the *chlops* moving along the path faded into the distance. Then I found I could move again. I got up stiffly and made my way back to the farm.

At the shelter the two *tatas* were waiting for me.

"The *chlops* are out looking for you," they said. "They told us that if they didn't find you, we were to bring you back to the village tonight."

I told them what had happened, but once again they didn't really believe me. *Ta* Bin said, "You must be hungry. I brought you some rice," and he gave me a big bag full.

I took it and began to eat ravenously, but he put his hand on my arm. "Don't wolf it all down. If you eat too much at once you'll be sick. Have a little at a time."

It was hard to eat just a handful, when for four days I'd had nothing but bamboo shoots and wild fruit, but I took his advice. I took a little food, waited a while, and then had some more. I began to feel stronger almost at once.

As I ate, *Ta* Chheng asked me where I had slept the night before. When I told him, he was clearly shocked: "No one dares to sleep there! Did you see the bad spirit?"

I told him what I had seen, and he believed me: he knew many people who told similar stories, but they had all died afterwards.

"I'm not afraid of evil spirits," I said. "I'm more afraid of the *chlops*. Evil spirits don't hit you from behind with a hoe, like the *chlops* who killed my family."

When the sun began to go down, the *tatas* gathered their belongings and prepared to go back to the village. I watched them in silence, and then got to my feet. I was sure that once we got back to the village the *chlops* would kill me, but I didn't really care. I'd had my bowl of rice, and now I was ready. The only possible purpose for living was to take revenge for my family, but I could see no way of achieving that. There was no point in staying in the jungle: I would starve or die of my injuries, and wild animals would eat me. I might as well have a quick death. Living was pain, from my broken body, from my mind and from my heart. I had suffered enough pain, so I marched back to the village to be executed by the *chlops*.

Darkness was falling as we approached the village, but in the dusk I saw a crowd of people waiting for me. I stiffened:

were they all going to join in my execution? Then I realised that people were calling my name: they came up to me and touched and hugged me; some of them were crying. I was utterly amazed: where were my killers, where were the people who had called me *khmang*, had hated and accused me? Some of them came and tied white threads on my wrists, a local practice to call the spirit back into a person, and they cried out in loud voices, asking my spirit to come back into me. They called me "the special one", "the resurrected one", and they brought me food and a clean shirt to put on. It wasn't the reception I had expected, and it reduced me to tears.

While I was eating, I realised that a message was being passed around: there was to be a special meeting. After my strange welcome, I hardly knew what to expect. The people gathered me up with them as they all moved over to the meeting shelter, and made me stand alone at the front. This was it, then, I thought. Now the final verdict will be given. I felt like a chicken waiting for slaughter.

Then a man named Mov stood up. "Don't let him die," he said. "His family are all dead. I'll take responsibility for him. He can be my foster son. I'll ensure that he doesn't take revenge: if he does, you can take my life." The leader looked around at the meeting. "Who agrees with Mov? Should he live?" I waited apprehensively for the answer, then I heard movement. All around me, the people were standing to signify their agreement: they supported Mov. They wanted me to live.

I couldn't believe what was happening. Why should a stranger put his life on the line for me? I didn't know Mov, and I didn't want to. If I was going to live, then my only reason for doing so was to exact vengeance for my family. How could I do that now Mov had staked his life for my good behaviour? I had promised on my family's grave that I would kill the *chlops* one day, and now this man would prevent me from doing it.

When the meeting was over, Mov came up and took me by the arm. He led me to his house and showed me where I was to sleep. "You're my foster son now," he said, "and I'll be your father."

It was hard for me to call him *pook* (father), because he wasn't my father. My only father was dead. Yet I owed this man my life: I had to accept him as he had offered to accept me. "I don't know why I stood up to defend you," he said. "I felt as though someone was telling me to save your life. But now I've done it. You'll be a son to me." I knelt in front of him and thanked him for saving me.

In the morning, *pook* Mov went out early, and came back carrying the roots of several plants. It turned out that he had some knowledge of herbal medicine. Although I hadn't told him about the pain in my chest, he seemed to know what was wrong. He boiled the roots and made a bitter medicine – it was hard to swallow, but I did as I was told. I wanted to get better. After a few days, my breathing became easier and the pain in my chest faded.

For the next week I stayed with *pook* Mov and his family – his wife, his five-year-old daughter and his three-year-old son. Mov and his wife treated me with the same care and affection they gave their own children, and they washed and bound my cuts and bruises until I began to recover. Then another village meeting was held: I stayed at home with the children while Mov and his wife attended. When they came back, they looked very upset. Mov put his arms around me and said, "I'm sorry, son. They've held another vote, and this time the leaders have decided you must die." He looked both sad and angry at the same time, but he knew he was helpless: he wasn't a leader, and what the *angkar loeu* decided became the law.

I knelt in front of him to show my respect. "*Pook*," I said, "I know you want to help me, but please don't risk it. You know you mustn't rebel against them. Even though you're an old-liberated person, they won't listen to you. I'm ready to die, in any case. I've had enough pain, and I don't want to suffer any more."

Then Mov hung his head. "Reaksa, you don't understand. They've chosen me to be the one to kill you. If I don't do it, they'll kill me. But I accepted you as my son. How can I kill you?"

It was a sad moment. I felt that I carried a burden of suffering, and now I'd brought it into this home where I had been welcomed and cared for, and made these kind people suffer too.

Mov sat down and ate his evening meal, but I couldn't eat anything. I knew I had survived death in the killing field, but perhaps it was right that my life was over. I was living a pretend life, in the wrong place and the wrong time. Mov would put it right and I would go to be with my family.

When he had finished eating, Mov picked up a hoe and an axe and led me through the village. He didn't tie me up, just led me in silence past the villagers who came out of their houses to watch us leave. Even outside the village he didn't speak to me, and I wondered what he was thinking. Would he club me from behind like the others did? From time to time I stole a glance at his face, but his expression told me nothing. We just walked together for hours into the jungle.

At last he stopped and turned to me: we were standing beside a large spiky bush.

"*Pook*," I said, "please do it now. I don't want to wait any longer. But please bury me properly, because I don't want my flesh to be torn by the wild animals the way my parents were."

Mov seemed to be trembling with emotion: he dropped the hoe and axe on the ground and put his arms around me. "I'm so afraid, my son. I know they'll kill me for this, but I can't kill you." Tears were running down his face. He brushed them away with his sleeve, turned away from me and bent down by the bush. To my astonishment, he pulled out a bulging sack, opened the top and started to empty it. Out came a pot, a big knife, a small bag of rice, a lighter, and a few other things. "I knew this might happen, so I came out a few days ago and put these things here. You should be able to live by yourself for a while. If you listen, you can hear a stream running over there to the west: it isn't far, and you'll be able to get fresh water there."

I was amazed: he'd prepared all these things and hidden them, and then led me back through the jungle to this place where he thought I could live. How could he be so caring and thoughtful, when my life might mean his own death?

"Now, hide yourself," he said. "I don't think anyone comes this way, but you mustn't let yourself be seen. I'll try to bring you more food soon: I'll leave it under this bush – the thorns will put anyone off from investigating too closely."

Before he left, he told me some more bad news: my older brothers were all dead, just as I had thought. "Don't worry about them," he told me. "Their troubles are over. You must hide and take care of yourself."

"*Pook*," I asked him, "what about you? How are you going to deal with the *angkar loeu*?" He hugged me and told me not to worry, then he turned and left, striding through the jungle with his axe and hoe. I wondered if he was walking home towards his death.

Once again I was alone in the jungle: free, but only to fight for my own survival. I was thirteen years old, too young for such a struggle. Once I was alone, I began to argue over the same old questions with myself. What was the point of living, with no family or friends left in the world? Living only meant remembering, remembering my own pain and grief, other people's pain, suffering, torture and execution. They were bad memories to be in the mind of a thirteen-year-old boy. Dying meant an end to suffering – yet when I thought about my foster father, I hesitated to give up.

When *pook* Mov took me into the jungle he could have killed me, he should have done so, but he didn't. Why had he tried, twice, to save me? Why had he risked his life for me yet again? What would he say to the villagers, and what would the *angkar loeu* do to him? I worried about him, and I knew that I'd have to try to survive for his sake. If he kept his word and came back with food, at least I'd know they hadn't killed him.

Life in the jungle was lonely, but I was much better off than before: my injuries were healing, and I had rice to eat. I kept busy, collecting water and finding extra food, by fishing and gathering wild berries and edible leaves. I was actually much more concerned about security than about food. I always moved stealthily, in case the *chlops* were around, and I found lots of good places where I could hide myself in a moment if anyone came along. At first I was scared of being alone in the jungle, but gradually I got used to the rustlings and calls of wild animals and birds. At least I had a little peace, more than I had when I lived in a village under the rule of the *chlops* and the Khmer Rouge. Life was difficult, but I was learning to survive.

After a month, my supplies of rice, salt and sugar ran out, so I went back to the thorn bush. Sure enough, my foster father had been true to his word: there was a big bag of rice and some salt. At least I knew now that he was alive, though

I had no idea how he had managed it, or how long the bag had been hidden there. Mov couldn't have known about my hiding-places, or he would have tried to speak to me. The only message I could leave him was to take the bag away: if he came back, he would guess that I had taken it, so he would know that I, too, was still alive.

Days, weeks, and months went by; it's hard to keep track of time in the jungle. I think it was about four months later when my situation became desperate again. The weather was bad, and it rained for days without stopping: my hideout was flooded and I couldn't find a dry place to sleep. I was ill, with pains in my chest and a rasping cough; I couldn't breathe properly, and sometimes blood ran from my nose. I didn't know what to do: I didn't know how to find the roots Mov had used to treat me before. Once again I felt sure that I was going to die soon. I tried to dig a grave for myself by the thorn bush: if my foster father came by, perhaps he would bury me properly. I knew that if I went back to the village they would execute me and give me a proper burial, but after all this time I wasn't so sure that I was willing to kneel and be killed. I would rather stay and take my chances in the jungle.

Early one morning I heard a voice calling my name: it was *pook* Mov. Although I had looked forward to seeing him, I hesitated to come out from my hiding-place: I had been away from people for too long, and I found it hard to trust anyone. He called for me and looked around for a while, then gave up and went home. The next morning he came back again, and this time I plucked up the courage to come out and speak to him.

"*Pook*," I said, "what are you doing here?" He was horrified when he saw me: my skin was yellow and I was terribly thin.

"Reaksa!" he cried, "I'm so glad to see you alive! I thought you might be ill. I knew you didn't have any covering against the rain, so I came looking for you."

"How are you?" I said. "Why didn't they kill you when you went back?"

"Things are better now," he said. "The village leader has been transferred out, and I've been assigned as a fisherman for our village. Come back to the village with me, and you can help me: we can go fishing together."

He also had good news about my sister Sopheap: she and her husband Chhounly were still alive! After our execution the *angkar loeu* sent a message to the leader of Sopheap's village, but the *chlop* there misread the message and killed someone else with the same name. I could hardly believe my ears – one of my family was still alive.

Despite all this good news, I was still unwilling to return to the village. Who knew what would happen when the people saw me? Twice I had left on my way to my death. Surely they'd want to finish me off this time.

Pook Mov and I sat together talking for a long time. In the end we agreed that I wouldn't go back with him. He would bring me some more herbal medicine, and some food, and I would go with him each day and help him catch fish for the village. So each day he drove his ox-cart to the lake, and I went with him to help with the fishing. In the evening, he took the fish back to the village and dropped me off by the edge of the jungle. My health improved with the regular food and medicine, and I began to look and feel much fitter.

Pook Mov kept trying to persuade me to return with him to the village, until the day he told me his work had been reassigned: he had to stay in the village to work, and he wouldn't be able to visit me in the jungle any more. Now, at last, I agreed to go back with him. I was tired of hiding in the jungle, and I had grown used to having my foster father's company. I didn't think I could bear the loneliness any more. My return was another strange experience: Mov had told the villagers I was alive, but once again they came out to touch and greet me, and once again they tied the white threads to my wrists: they obviously thought that I was a special person to have escaped death at least twice: I needed help to keep my spirit from escaping.

Once I was settled in the village, I began to realise that I didn't behave like other children. At first I thought I was just having a hard time adjusting to life in a community. I wasn't used to having so many people around. I was tired, but I couldn't sleep; I shivered constantly with nervousness, and I couldn't concentrate on what people said to me. I was always reliving the events of the execution in my head, but I was used to that – I hardly thought about it. I just knew it would never leave me. Now I know there's a label for my condition: Post-Traumatic Stress Disorder.

I was sent to work with the old-liberated children's team – there were no new-liberated people left in the village for me to work with. Because I lived with my foster father, my classification had changed: now I was an old-liberated person too. Every week I had to attend a meeting with the other children: it was always full of talk about how lazy and useless the new-liberated children had been – even though they were all dead. They also proclaimed that there were no more *khmangs* of the *angkar loeu*. They said they had all been destroyed, conveniently forgetting that I had once been labelled as one of them. I was sick of hearing this talk, but I had to learn to ignore it.

Besides working with the children's team I also helped my foster father and his wife; I appreciated all they had done for me, and the risks they had taken. In my free time I went fishing for more food for the family, just as I had for my real family.

I worked hard to prove that I wasn't lazy as they'd been told all new-liberated people were.

I found it hard to go on living in the village. The rest of the villagers carried on with their lives as though nothing had happened, as though the people who had lived and worked among them, and then suddenly disappeared into the killing fields, were of no account. Even though they had welcomed me back from the jungle like one returned from the dead, that didn't change their attitude to me. Many of them called me "Chinese" boy – as an insult – and said I was useless. Even though I was officially now one of the old-liberated people, I knew they could kill me at any time if they chose to do so, and nothing would be said. The only person who seemed to care for me was my foster father: I had no other friends in the village, and Mov had made himself unpopular by taking me in. My late father used to say, "A bad person has good friends and a good person has many enemies." That was true for me. I knew I was constantly under scrutiny: the least mistake, the smallest sign of laziness or unwillingness to work for the Khmer Rouge cause, and I would be denounced to the *angkar loeu*.

My father used to say, "Listen to three words and answer with only one." He meant that it wasn't safe to say much, especially with the *chlops* listening. I learned my lesson well: I pretended to be deaf whenever I was insulted and abused. I knew that if I reacted, I would probably be killed. It was hard to face all this without my real family around me. I tried to remember everything my parents had taught me, but deep in my heart I was desperately lonely and filled with grief.

One day I had a strange experience: I had driven the water-buffalo cart into the jungle to collect wood for the family. I filled the cart with wood and turned the buffaloes for home, but for some reason they stopped in their tracks and refused to go any further. I prodded them with my stick, I shouted at them, and I went round to their heads and pulled at their harness, but I couldn't get them to move. Their eyes were rolling in fear: I thought perhaps a wild animal had scared them, but I couldn't see anything.

Then I heard someone calling my name, "Reaksa, Reaksa."

I was sure I'd heard that voice before. I peered into the trees but I couldn't see anybody. The buffaloes had knelt down on the path, which unnerved me even more: if there had been an animal around they would have been ready to run.

Then the voice came again, and this time I recognised it: my brother Pinith, who had been sent away a year ago to work with the youth mobile team. He was calling me but I couldn't see him.

"Brother!" I shouted. "Come out! Please come out! I want to see you!"

Then I realised the truth, and started to cry. However much I begged him to come out and show his face, no one appeared. I knew he was dead – my foster father had told me so. I was speaking to his spirit. Was I going mad? The buffaloes were still kneeling, as though they, too, could sense the presence of my brother. I was overcome by grief all over again, and I sat on the cart and wept for my dead family for almost an hour. Then in desperation I said, "*Bong*, if you're really here, please let me go. I miss you so much but I want you to go in peace now." At once the feeling of someone watching me went away, and the water buffaloes stood up and began pulling again.

When I got home I told my foster father what had happened. I think he believed me, but he didn't encourage me to talk about it. There were too many dead in Cambodia in those days – too many spirits might be lurking in the jungle. That night I couldn't sleep at all: my strange experience had stirred up my feelings yet again. I wished I could see Pinith one more time, but I knew it was impossible.

Shortly after this I met a young man on the path just outside our village. He said to me, "Are you Piney's brother? The one who was executed and escaped from the grave?"

I was shocked; no one had ever asked me such a thing before. The people in my village took care not to mention what had happened to me. After a moment I replied, "Yes, I am."

"Are you Reaksa?" he asked.

"Yes," I said. "How did you know? How did you know Piney?"

"I knew you because you look so much like him," he replied. "Piney and I were good friends. My name's Thorn."

I remembered the name: Piney used to tell me how kind *mith* Thorn had been when they were sent away to work together. *Mith* Thorn lived about four miles away, so I was surprised to see him so near to our home. He said he had something to tell me, so we walked along together, but he seemed to find it hard to speak. After a few minutes he said, "I don't know how to tell you this, but I must. I'm the one who killed your brother."

I couldn't hear anything more: furious rage boiled up in me, blocking my ears to his words. If I could have hurt him, I would: I would have smashed him into a million pieces. I clenched my fists until my nails dug into my palms, but I knew it was useless. *Mith* Thorn towered over me: he was an adult, and I was only a little boy. He could hold me off with one hand.

He saw my face, and said, "I know you're angry with me, but I want you to understand. I didn't want to do it. I had no choice. They ordered me to kill him, and if I didn't, they would have killed me."

I told him I didn't want to hear any more, but he said, "Please hear me out. I need to tell you. Piney and I were planning to run away to Thailand, but I think the Khmer Rouge soldiers in charge of our group must have guessed. They arrested Piney before we could get away. They took us into the jungle, pointed a gun at my head and made me dig a grave. Then they ordered me to kill him. I closed my eyes and clubbed your brother's head from behind with a hoe. Then I buried him there." He broke down in tears, and I didn't catch the next few words. I stayed silent, listening.

Mith Thorn lifted his head and said, "Ever since that day, I haven't known what to do. I can't sleep: every night I see Piney's face; I hear him calling my name. I miss him, and I can't live with my guilt. Can you forgive me? If you want to take revenge for his death by killing me, I won't stop you."

This was my chance. I might be weak and small, but here was my brother's killer, saying I could take my revenge, and he wouldn't resist. I had promised on my family's grave that I would avenge their deaths. Now the killing could start.

I looked up at *mith* Thorn, a grown man standing on the path in front of me, with his head bowed and tears pouring down his face. I knew how the evil system worked: the Khmer Rouge guessed he was plotting to leave, but they didn't want to kill him, one of the old-liberated people. They could kill my brother, though, a man of no account, one of the worthless people. And they could order Thorn to do it; if he refused to kill his closest friend, he had rebelled against their orders, and then they had an excuse to kill him, too. How could I blame him?

"Why do you want to tell me this terrible story?" I asked him.

He replied, "I thought if I came to ask your forgiveness, I might not hear his voice calling to me every night."

"Can you tell me where his grave is?"

He told me the grave was in the jungle to the west of his village; he had visited it himself, in secret. He added, "One day, if the political situation changes, we may be free to go where we want. If that happens, I'll take you there to see it for yourself."

What could I say to him? How could I ever forgive him? I stood in silence, and after a while, Thorn turned away from me and went off along the path. I never saw him again.

CHAPTER SEVEN

FULFILLING MY LAST PROMISE

*"By faith he made his home in the promised land like a
stranger in a foreign country."* (Hebrews 11:9)

In December 1978 Cambodia was invaded by Vietnam. Pol
Pot, the Communist leader, was removed from his position
and a new government was set up. None of this was of much
interest to a thirteen-year-old, but I was aware that Cambodia
had entered a new era. The Vietnamese army, invading from
the east, drove all the Khmer Rouge soldiers westward into the
jungles bordering Thailand. Cambodia was liberated and so
was I. When the Khmer Rouge soldiers had gone, I knew that
a hated and evil power was gone from our village. The country
was still communist, but the communes were breaking up and
the Vietnamese encouraged people to return to their homes.
All the divisions of new-liberated and old-liberated were gone:
now we were all just Cambodians again.

Only two other members of my family had survived the
Khmer Rouge's reign of terror: my sister Sopheap and her
husband Chhounly. Now that it was safe to travel, Chhounly
came to the village to collect me; he said I could go and live
with them in the city. It was wonderful to see him, but I told

him I couldn't go back with him at once. I wanted to stay with my foster father for a while, to help him support his family, and show him my respect and gratitude for all he had done for me. He had saved my life on more than one occasion, and without his help, I could not have survived.

I stayed in the village for another year before going to live with Sopheap and Chhounly in the town of Kompong Thkov, about 50 kilometres from the city of Siemreap. We settled down well together, and tried as best we could to get on with our lives. We knew, however, that there was one duty we still had to fulfil: we needed to give our family a proper burial.

Chhounly came with me to look for the mass grave in the jungle where the bones of my parents, my brothers and sisters, and all the other victims lay. It wasn't hard to find, because I don't think I could ever forget that journey from the village to the place of execution. But we arrived to find a shocking scene. Animals had dug into the loose earth; the ground was disturbed and bones were scattered all around. There was no way anyone could tell one body from another; everything was gone.

I knelt by the grave once more, and wept for the poor broken bodies, desecrated in death as they had been despised in life. I told my family that I wanted to take their bones away with me, to bury them in a pagoda, where the proper prayers could be said. Then I bowed three times and collected all the bones I could find. We made a hot fire and cremated them there in the jungle, because we couldn't have carried so many bones away. Then we wrapped the ashes in a white cloth and carried them home. I took them to a pagoda near our home, called Wat Tapon, and asked the Buddhist monks there to pray for them. On special Buddhist feast days I went there to grieve for them, lighting candles and incense for their departed spirits; it was all I could do. My three older brothers had been killed in different places, and I couldn't find their graves, but I swore I would never forget them.

Now we had done all we could to pay our last respects to our family, and I knew it was time to move on. I moved back to the city of Siemreap, and lived with my aunt so that I could go back to school; I had missed about five years of schooling during the Khmer Rouge's regime. At first I thought this would be a way back into normal life: my aunt's family would welcome me and I would try to study, get a job, and be part of the new Cambodian society that was forming itself in the new political climate.

Things weren't so easy, though. For one thing, there was my own mental state. I found it hard to concentrate at school: I had been away from books and normal life for a long time. I was also in a state of constant distress: the trauma I had suffered wasn't going to be easily forgotten. I was depressed, nervous, irritable, and confused. I would go into extended daydreams in which I relived moments of fear and pain: falling out of a tree in the forest; kneeling for my own execution; climbing out of a mass grave covered in blood. I would have flashbacks in which I would hear the thump of a club on my baby brother's head, or see Sopheak's face as he was hung on the fence and tortured.

Perhaps I could have recovered if there had been any help for me, but no one in Cambodia in those days understood the condition. There were no trained psychologists or counsellors to guide me, and no doctors to treat me. Even my surviving family didn't understand. Theirs was a Buddhist society, and Buddhism has only one understanding of suffering: it is a result of "karma". Buddhists believe in reincarnation: that the soul goes through a constant cycle of birth, death and rebirth. What happens to you in your life is a result of what you did in previous lives. So if bad things happen to you now, it is your own responsibility, because you did bad things in a previous life. It is a law of cause and effect. So people saw me as a poor unfortunate boy who had done evil things in a previous life, and deserved the pain and suffering inflicted upon me in this life.

I could have no standing in this society because of my karma; as soon as people knew what had happened to me, they judged me. Once again I was a victim because of what the Khmer Rouge regime had done to me. As a result, I became even more withdrawn: I was living in a community but I didn't feel part of it. There was no comfort for me here.

Four years went by, and I left school and decided to join the police force. I admit that I had only one motive: to fulfil my first promise to my family. I would take revenge for their deaths, and seek out and kill those who murdered them. I enjoyed visualising what I would do to them: I would torture them as they had tortured little Sopheak. I would cut their bodies into little pieces, and pour soy sauce onto their flesh. I wanted to see them suffer.

However, only a month after I became a policeman, I received a letter from my mother's uncle, asking me to visit him. When I met him, I realised that he knew why I had joined the police force. He kept lecturing me on one subject: forgiveness. He said that killing people didn't solve anything, and making others suffer didn't solve the problem of our own suffering. I didn't argue with him, but I was angry in my heart. What did he know of my feelings? When I left, he asked me to make him a promise – that I wouldn't take revenge. I had to show him respect, even though I disagreed with him, and so I agreed. I didn't intend to forgive anyone, but I agreed not to kill anyone. Making this promise to the old man made me terribly unhappy: how could I fulfil my promise to my dead family and also my promise to him?

A short while later I happened to come across one of the Khmer Rouge who had ordered the *chlops* to kill my family. In my position as a policeman, I was able to arrest him. Now I had the power: this time, I was the one with the gun. Given this opportunity, I knew I was going to break my promise to my great-uncle, though the thought made me uneasy. I laid my plans carefully: first I deliberately got drunk – I had to do that to suppress my feelings of guilt. Then I dragged the man into the forest and took out my gun. The man begged me not to kill him: he said that he had been ordered by the *angkar loeu* to take part in the executions. If he disobeyed, he would have been killed. I was reminded of *mith* Thorn, who had said the same thing. I had believed him; could I believe this man, too? My finger tightened on the trigger, but I seemed to hear my great-uncle's voice again: killing him wouldn't remove my pain. I closed my eyes and tried again, but my fingers just wouldn't work. Killing one man wouldn't make me feel better. Killing a whole village wouldn't end my anger. As my hand dropped, I realised that I couldn't do it. I'd had the chance to avenge my family, and I had failed. I could not fulfil my first promise.

Later I heard that the man was dead: he was killed by someone else. Some other survivor had exacted the revenge I was unable to take.

These events made me even more disillusioned. I had joined the police force with only one intention: to use my position to get revenge. Now I knew I couldn't do it, I lost interest in my job. My life was meaningless. I thought of my second promise, to become a Buddhist monk, and I knew that was also beyond my power, for the current regime still didn't allow young men to become monks. I went to the pagoda where I had buried my family, knelt and prayed to them.

"Parents, brothers and sisters, please forgive me. Grant me peace, even though I can't fulfil my promises. There's nothing left for me in the country of my birth. I'm going to try to leave."

On 16th April 1984, after the Khmer New Year, I decided to go to Thailand. It was a dangerous undertaking: Cambodians were still not allowed to leave the country. Any attempt to escape would be considered an act of betrayal, punishable by imprisonment. I asked the police commissioner for permission to take a few days' leave to visit my sister, and he agreed. It would be a few days before my absence was noticed.

The night before I left I wrote two letters, one to my sister and the other to my aunt's family. I told them I felt I could no longer live in Cambodia, for life there was meaningless for me. I said I was sorry I couldn't come and say goodbye in person, but I wanted to escape. I left the letters in my pillow.

In those days, long after the overthrow of the Khmer Rouge regime, fighting was still going on. The Vietnamese army was being resisted by the remnants of the Khmer Rouge and by the guerrilla forces of Prince Sihanouk, who had been head of state until 1970. Cambodia was still in a state of upheaval, and crossing the battle zones was dangerous. The countryside was littered with land mines and booby traps, so even walking across unfamiliar fields could be a matter of life and death.

I travelled with two couples who also wished to escape to Thailand. Once we were stopped by government soldiers, but fortunately they only wanted money: when we gave them some they let us pass, first warning us about the local minefields. Then we entered the Khmer Resistance Zone, and at once we were arrested by more soldiers, this time from the other side. They thought we were spies for the Vietnamese, and they took us into their office and interrogated us one by one. When it was my turn, one of them pointed a gun to my head while the other one raped my friend's wife. I couldn't believe my eyes. Here I was, trying to escape from my past, from a childhood destroyed by the Khmer soldiers, and I had walked right back into their power and into the same cruelty as before. These men were supposed to be fighting the Vietnamese, but they were once again torturing their own people.

It was like going back in time: yet again I had to suppress my anger and revulsion, for I knew they wouldn't hesitate to kill me if I spoke out. They questioned and stripped me, but they found nothing, and eventually they let me go on my way to the refugee camp.

We walked for two days before we reached Rithysen Camp, and when we arrived I wondered why we had come. It was a hellish place. The United Nations organisation was providing food for only the women and children, so the men had to find work – most of them joined the resistance just to get food. I managed to get a job working for a high ranking military officer in the camp, so I was able to eat. I wrote letters to some cousins in the United States, and they sent me money and urged me to go to the Khao I Dang camp, less than ten miles over the border in Thailand. I paid a guide to lead me through the dangerous border crossing: many people were gunned down as they tried to escape.

I arrived in Thailand in November 1984 – not a moment too soon. The government knew that the Rithysen camp was a source of men joining the resistance army, and a month after I left they destroyed the camp completely. All the refugees there were split up and sent to other camps nearby.

At first I had to hide out in Khao I Dang: I didn't have a UNHCR (United Nations High Commission for Refugees) number, so I was an "illegal" refugee – I had no food to eat and nowhere to stay. I was always afraid that soldiers would come and send me back to the Khmer Rouge. One day some Thai soldiers did come and arrest me, but I managed to escape, and not long afterwards the UNHCR officers arrived to sort out the administration and give us all a number. I was now a "legal" refugee and no longer needed to fear arrest.

I lived in the Khao I Dang camp for five years. It wasn't an easy time, and I battled constantly with depression. Even though I had work, and food, and safety, life seemed pointless. Khao I Dang camp was vast: there were over 120,000 people there. Among them was a group of Cambodian Christians, who worshipped together every day. They moved around the camp, telling everyone who would listen about Jesus Christ's love and forgiveness. I wasn't interested. All I could think about was going to the United States to live with my cousin and starting a new life. Buddhism hadn't helped me in my distress, so why should any other religion help me? I didn't want the lifeline of faith: I wanted to survive on my own. I didn't have time or energy for God; I didn't want to be led in his way. I preferred my own way, even though that meant anger, and helplessness, and misery. I closed my heart to everything they said. "If God is so good and powerful, why did he allow the Khmer Rouge to kill my family?" I would ask. "If I received Jesus Christ as my Lord and Saviour, would my family come back to me?" I shut out every thought about God.

I waited a long time for an interview with the American INS (Immigration and Naturalization Service) but in the end they rejected my application. The loss of this hope, which had sustained me for years, filled me with fresh despair. I couldn't sleep, I couldn't eat, and I felt as though I was drowning in depression, sinking deeper and deeper until finally I ran out of energy to swim. I felt as though I was dead inside. I was very hopeless. Hopelessness was the greatest enemy of my life.

Only then did I give up and admit that I needed help – from God. At last I recognised the need for something outside myself to restore my bruised, battered spirit and give me some hope. I was crying out for help, and my soul was hungry for peace. I remembered some words the Christians used to say when they prayed together: "And the peace of God, which transcends all understanding, will guard your hearts and your minds in Christ Jesus" (Philippians 4:7). That was what I needed: someone to give me peace and protect my soul from the black despair that always seemed to be waiting to pull me down.

So I prayed, "Lord God, I've battled enough for my life. I can't carry on any longer in my own strength. I'm tired of my life and I need your help. I want to leave this country and go to live in Canada. If I'm accepted to live there, I will believe in you. . . ."

Then I wrote letters to the Canadian Embassy in Thailand, asking for refuge in Canada. In November 1988 a Canadian immigration officer came to interview me at the refugee centre in Aranyaprathet, and early the following year I received a letter. I was accepted! My freedom was ensured at last.

This was my first hint that God was powerful and good: how fast he had answered my prayer! I was transferred to a transit camp at Phanatnikhom for lessons about the Canadian way of life. I was full of excitement: Canada looked to me like a land of opportunity, peace and hope. I knew my life could begin again in that place, and I was sure God had a purpose in sending me there.

On 15th May 1989 I arrived at Pearson Airport in Toronto, and was taken to the World Vision Reception Centre (WVRC). At first everything was strange: the language, the buildings, the faces of the people. But I was most astonished by the staff at the centre. They looked after me and loved me as if I was one of them, and their actions showed me clearly that Christians are different from other people. I had never been among people who accepted me for myself, and who didn't believe that I had brought my suffering on myself. For the first time, I began to feel free of guilt.

It was while I was there that I began to understand more about the love of Jesus Christ. I met a young student of political science, Chuck Ferguson, who worked for World Vision Canada. He took care of me and prayed for me, and taught me about the life and death and resurrection of Jesus. When I found a room of my own to rent, Chuck gave me a Bible of my own, and invited me to read the Gospel of John. I loved what I read. Here was a God who shared in his people's sufferings and understood them. The idea of a God who cared about my pain touched my heart.

Being able to trust in a loving God transformed my life. I was leaving behind the bondage of Khmer Buddhism with its constant struggle to earn merit for the next life. Now I knew that I could have eternal life with God, and the price for my sins had already been paid – by Jesus. I could work and devote my whole life to his service, but it was service freely given, a loving return for his gift of life, not a desperate attempt to improve my own karma. I could also leave behind the superstitious religion of the peasants, the constant fear of the shadowy world of spirits, with its lurking demons and the restless ghosts of dead ancestors. God had power over every spirit of darkness and evil, and he cared for me: it was like coming out into the sunlight after being in a dark place. I knew I could believe in Jesus as my Lord and Saviour, and I committed myself to give my life to him. He is the only true God, who gives me life and hope. Since that time my heart has been filled with joy, and life has meaning for me once again. He is the Prince of Peace indeed.

During my first year in Canada, I was supported by the Canadian government: they gave me $600 a month to live on. I was supposed to go to lessons to learn the language, but I found that my English was already too advanced for the class I was assigned to, so I asked the immigration office for permission to get a job and start supporting myself. They were happy about this, so I got a job: first in a plastics factory, and then, later, with the Canadian Cambodian Association in Toronto. This was a wonderful move, because I was able to help other refugees who arrived in Canada as I had done.

After some months I decided to go back to school, so in September 1990 I enrolled at Tyndale College, to study for the degree of Bachelor of Religious Studies. I funded my education with a scholarship and a small government loan, which I paid back by working at different jobs in the vacations: as a cleaner, a counsellor and a sociological researcher. It was wonderful to be studying again: with peace in my heart I could concentrate much better on what I was learning. Studying the Bible helped me to learn more about Jesus and about my new faith, and the extra courses in social science gave me a greater understanding of the world around me and of my place in it.

I got to know the other students and began to make friendships again; one of those friends was Phil Ulrich. His mother, Carolyn Ulrich, became my foster mother. She has been wonderful to me, taking an interest in all I do and loving me just like a mother. Although she lived some distance away, we always kept in touch by letter and phone, and she always prayed for me, especially when I was under pressure from my work. She even encouraged me not to work too hard, and told me to take time off from my studies for leisure and relaxation. After completing my first degree in 1993 I went on to Providence Theological Seminary to take a masters degree in Counselling and Christian Education: when I graduated in

May 1996, Carolyn came to my graduation as she had promised. I was thrilled to have "Mom" at my graduation, like the other students. I felt that a little part of my family had been restored to me.

CHAPTER EIGHT

LIFE AFTER LOSS

"If you have a knife, you can't use it to cut its own handle. You need to find another knife to cut it."
Cambodian saying.

In the years after I lost my family I developed all the characteristic symptoms of psychological distress. I felt guilty about having survived while my family perished, and not having been able to help them. Every night I went to bed feeling terribly depressed, and then had difficulty in sleeping. When I woke up in the morning, I felt sad and hopeless. Why had I survived? Death seemed attractive, because I would never feel depressed again. Every day, images from those years of torturous existence filled my mind; I tried to control them, but without success. I asked myself constantly why I wanted to live, with my world gone for ever and nothing left to live for. Sadness was the major component of my life.

Psychological trauma causes feelings of intense fear, helplessness and loss of self-control, and the response is complex, involving both body and mind. The sense of threat causes an adrenalin rush: the sufferer goes into a state of alert every time he relives the imagined danger. This made me restless and uneasy: I couldn't stick at a task or sit still for any length of time. I was anxious and irritable; I felt ill; I couldn't function normally. I couldn't remember what I tried to learn, what I said to friends, or even what I had done the day before.

Long after I was safe, I went on reliving the trauma: it became encoded in an abnormal form of memory, which broke spontaneously into my consciousness, as flashbacks during the day and in my dreams at night. For years my sleep was constantly interrupted by nightmares, from which I would awake sweating and shaking all over. Sometimes I dreamed of being chased and bludgeoned by the Khmer Rouge. The first night I spent alone in the jungle I had dreamed that an evil *chlop* was chasing me, and in my sleep I struggled until I fell out of the tree. This dream became fixed in my subconscious, and I dreamed it again and again. Later on, when I was staying in the refugee camp on the Thai border, I was constantly afraid that soldiers would come and arrest me, and these dreams recurred too. No wonder I was afraid to fall asleep.

To protect myself I tried hard not to think about what had happened – I shut out any thoughts about my family, and avoided anything that might remind me of them. I lost trust in myself and in others. I longed for comfort and friendship, but I was terribly afraid: if I loved someone else, I might lose them, too. My capacity for intimacy with other people was inhibited by these intense and contradictory feelings of need and fear. I felt like a different person from the carefree, friendly boy of my early years. When I went back to live with my sister and my aunt, they complained that I had changed. I avoided old friends and shut myself off emotionally from any kind of affection. I was alive but I felt numb, as though I were dead. The traumas I had lived through didn't only damage my body and my mind; they also damaged my ability to relate to other people socially. This made me very lonely, because I refused to risk any social or emotional contacts.

When I started to study at Tyndale College, I took an Introduction to Psychology course, and that was when I realised that I was suffering from Post-Traumatic Stress Disorder (PTSD). I spent a lot of time studying this condition, but my knowledge made no difference. I refused to seek help from a psychologist or psychiatrist because I didn't feel I could trust anybody. I was sure they couldn't help me. Perhaps my scepticism resulted from the belief that no one in Canada could have any idea of what I had gone through. They had never experienced anything like it: their knowledge was derived from theories and academic literature on the subject. I felt more comfortable talking to other Cambodians than to psychologists; I could connect with them, and relate their experiences to my own.

I began to do my own research into PTSD, and discovered several theories about its treatment, but I still had no idea how to deal with the crisis in my own life. It seemed to me that PTSD could not be healed, but only managed. My research unearthed descriptions of how victims of non-combat-related trauma, such as myself, behaved. Psychologists believed the best way to help was to challenge the victim to confront memories of the trauma and to express the painful emotions associated with it; the aim was to move towards regaining self-control and a sense of competence and self-worth. Nowadays more treatment options have been developed including group therapy, hypnosis, and even some drug therapies.

Armed with the results of my research, I knew I should seek professional help, but I couldn't bring myself to do it. There is a Cambodian saying, "If you have a knife, you can't use it to cut its own handle. You need to find another knife to cut it." In other words, you can't treat yourself. Yet I still could not trust the professionals enough to put myself in their hands, so I tried to deal with it on my own. I searched out other Cambodian nationals who had fled to Canada, who had some experience of what life was like under the Khmer Rouge. Many of them had seen atrocities like those I had witnessed, and many had lost members of their families: in a population of around seven million, at least two million died in those years, so scarcely a family was left untouched.

I found that it helped me to talk to them. Because they shared my experiences, I felt less alone. I also found that simply making myself talk about these things somehow controlled the memories, and articulating the emotions made them more manageable. Then I tried another technique of talking to myself in front of a mirror. In private, I could say things I still couldn't bring myself to tell other people. At first I found this really difficult: the pain was too great. But I forced myself to go on because it was a way of learning to trust myself. As I slowly grew more in touch with my emotions – emotions I had tried to bury and hide – it grew easier.

Sometimes I used a tape recorder, and recorded the most difficult questions: "Reaksa, what did you see the Khmer Rouge do to your family?" "If you had the power, what would you do to them?" I made myself listen to the questions and reply to them, looking in a mirror, forcing myself to see the reality of my condition. I worked on this over a period of two years, and I seemed to see an improvement. In my conscious life, at least, I was managing better, growing less emotionally numb and reducing the intrusion of the daily flashbacks.

Nightmares were a different problem, however. When I went to bed, my soul still felt full of despair. It was then that I began to meditate on the Bible, and I found in the Book of Psalms a wonderful source of support and comfort. Here was someone like me who had known despair, and who was not afraid to cry out to God in pain and anguish. Across the centuries I heard the voice of a man who wept and cried to his God, and yet who always reaffirmed the reality of God's ability to hold him safe.

Give me relief from my distress; be merciful to me and hear my prayer . . . I will lie down and sleep in peace, for you alone, O Lord, make me dwell in safety. (Psalm 4:1,8)

On the wicked he will rain fiery coals and burning sulphur; a scorching wind will be their lot. For the Lord is righteous, he loves justice. (Psalm 11:6,7)

My heart is glad and my tongue rejoices; my body also will rest secure, because you will not abandon me to the grave. (Psalm 16:9,10)

When evil men advance against me to devour my flesh . . . they will stumble and fall . . . For in the day of trouble he will keep me safe in his dwelling . . . lead me in a straight path because of my oppressors . . . I will see the goodness of the Lord in the land of the living. (Psalm 27:2,5,11,13)

You will not fear the terror of night . . . For he will command his angels concerning you to guard you in all your ways. (Psalm 91:5,11)

I have stilled and quietened my soul; like a weaned child with its mother. (Psalm 131:2)

I read a psalm every day, and as I read, my trust in God's goodness and power was strengthened. I felt more secure. Psalm 23 became my favourite: whenever I read it, I felt safe in the presence of God. The psalm begins with David, King of Israel, comparing himself to a sheep while God himself is the faithful, diligent shepherd. He feeds the sheep in a pleasant pasture full of rich grass and abundant water; nothing they need is lacking.

> The Lord is my shepherd, I shall not be in want.
> He makes me lie down in green pastures,
> he leads me beside quiet waters,
> he restores my soul. (Psalm 23:1–3)

As I put my confident trust in God, I knew that he could restore my soul, and give me the peace I craved. I was being led by God to a place where I could rest in his care and protection.

> He guides me in paths of righteousness
> for his name's sake.
> Even though I walk through the valley of the shadow of death,
> I will fear no evil,
> for you are with me;
> your rod and your staff,
> they comfort me. (Psalm 23:3–4)

Life is still difficult, but I know that I'm guided by God, and this gives me the courage to face the challenges of each day. Nightmares still lurk, but I know that God's protection, the shepherd's rod and staff, are all the assurance my soul needs.

> You prepare a table before me in the presence of my enemies.
> You anoint my head with oil;
> my cup overflows.
> Surely goodness and love will follow me all the days of my life,
> and I will dwell in the house of the Lord for ever. (Psalm 23: 5–6)

I might never lose the sense of the presence of my enemies, but this affirmation of God's goodness reassures me. In this context I can pray about my fear, trusting in God's love and protection.

This psalm was also special to me in another way. One night when I was meditating on it, I seemed to see a picture of the cross with a ray of light on it. I didn't know how I saw the picture, but it was very real to me. I told some friends about this vision, and they said it was some kind of illusion, but I knew it was real. It was another source of comfort and reassurance.

Since I've been using this psalm for evening meditation, my nightmares have left me: I haven't once dreamed about being hunted by the Khmer Rouge or the Thai soldiers. It seems as though my need for security and comfort while I sleep is met by this psalm, because I know I can trust God. I told some psychologists how I'd learned to deal with my nightmares by this method, and they didn't believe me. I admit that it doesn't sound very scientific, but I don't care. I tried the scientific advice, and it didn't work; the Book of Psalms does work, and that's good enough for me.

It has worked for others, too. I have worked with many Cambodians who display all the symptoms of PTSD that I once had, and I have taught them the use of Psalm 23. Many of them have told me that it deals with their nightmares, and helps them to feel secure in the presence of the Lord.

Another aspect of my recovery was dealing with grief. In Cambodian culture, like many others, crying is not acceptable for men. "Real men don't cry." "Big boys don't cry." "Crying is a sign of weakness." I hardly ever saw a Cambodian man crying. When I was alone in the jungle, I cried freely for my family, but once I was back in society, I knew I would have to suppress my tears, and there was no release for the emotional tension I lived with every day.

It was years before I realised that this was an unhealthy convention, which controlled my behaviour for no good reason. I was coming to see that my sorrow, guilt, depression, anger, loneliness, anxiety and shame were all emotionally normal, aspects of a grief that seemed almost too deep to bear. If I was going to recover from the psychological distress I was suffering, I had to voice my grief openly and honestly. I didn't need to suppress my emotions – in fact, it took a great deal of courage to allow them to surface.

Tears are not a sign of weakness, but of healing: crying releases emotional tension. For me it was a sign that I was beginning to accept the reality of my loss, and also to acknowledge that my loss was worthy of grief. That meant enduring real feelings of sadness and anger and assuming full responsibility for my own feelings.

Crying took emotional energy, but I couldn't do it to order. When a friend said to me, "You've been through such a lot. Why don't you cry? It'll release the pain," I felt very angry. What did he know about crying? He didn't understand my pain. Was he trying to make me cry so that *he* could feel better? I didn't cry then.

When I did cry, I locked myself in my room, and set myself to recall all the good times I had when my family was alive. Then I remembered the bad times, like the hours I spent sitting and grieving by their newly covered grave. That was when the tears came, and I accepted that the family was gone for ever. Sometimes I dreamed of us having a good time, laughing together as a family or playing with the new baby. When I woke up and realised it wasn't real, I cried again. Some people might think that indulging in tears in this way wasn't very healthy, but for me it felt safe. Alone in my room I could cry for as long as I wanted, I could beat my pillow and let my pain escape. It was another step in trusting myself and my emotions.

Dealing with grief became very important: it was the core of my sadness, and I found different ways of exposing it. One way was through music – sitting relaxed and listening to certain pieces I could let the tears flow. Another way was to talk to people with similar experiences. Sometimes we would be able to weep together, and that helped us both. When I talked about the loss of my family to Elizabeth Davey, the English professor at Tyndale College, she didn't say anything at first: she just looked at me and her eyes filled with tears. After a few minutes, she told me that she had suffered a bereavement not long before. I knew that she felt for me, and I wept too: I felt very comfortable crying with her. Those who have experienced grief are often the best counsellors: they seem to know instinctively the right words to say and the right time to say them.

Another way in which I dealt with grief was by writing letters of farewell to my family. This was hard, but like my other methods, the effort was worth it: it made me feel closer to them, yet able to absorb their loss. It took me a long time to formulate the words I wanted to say. In the end I wrote:

Dear parents and brothers and sisters,

It's very painful for me to live without all of you. My heart is always empty. Sometimes I feel as though my legs and hands have been cut off. I want to come to you, but I can't. Without you my world has been destroyed. I miss the joy of the life we lived together. You are gone for ever, and I will never see any of you again, but I will always remember you in my heart and my tears. There are so many things I'd like to tell you, but I can't write them down. I'm writing this letter to say the words I never wanted to say in life, but I have to. Goodbye to all of you. I wish you could hear me.

With love,
Reaksa

The word I found hardest to write or say was "goodbye". It reminded me of the three terrible days I spent sitting by the mass grave, when I said it over and over again. I hadn't wanted to leave, and when I finally walked away, I knew I would never see my family again.

For a long time afterwards I found it hard to say goodbye to a close friend or a loved one. When I finished my graduate studies, my foster mother, Carolyn Ulrich, flew a thousand miles to attend my graduation ceremony. We had two happy days together, talking non-stop until I took her back to the airport for her flight home. We stood at the gate, and I waited for her to say the word first, but she didn't: she just hugged me with tears in her eyes, and went off to board her plane. I was troubled by the fact that I hadn't said goodbye to her.

A week later I received a letter from her. She wrote:

I hope you didn't think I was being distant, but saying goodbye is always hard. It's a time when I say very little and always those little bitty tears let me down. I felt sad for you, for I sensed your deep sorrow that day, for the family you no longer have. I know that no one can feel what you have gone through, or fill the void inside you. But God spared you, as a young boy, for a special purpose, and he can and will make you strong because of your loss and sorrow. You need never forget your family, but let God continue to heal your mind. Let him help you through all the small things in your life, and he will lead you through the big hurdles that seem impossible.

It was a wonderful letter, and it comforted me to realise that other people find goodbyes difficult as well. It took me a few weeks to write a goodbye letter to her.

My final way of dealing with grief was very simple, because it involved the standard prescription for stress: I learned to exercise regularly and sleep well. I took up jogging, walking, and playing tennis – it was all very helpful and seemed to release yet more of the tension inside me, and the physical exertion helped me to sleep. In all, I learned to take care of myself. Grief isn't something I can avoid, so I have to learn to live with it, and keeping myself healthy gives me the best chance of doing so.

As I slowly began to recover from my psychological trauma, to deal with the physical, mental and emotional effects of my experiences, another aspect began to appear: my anger and desire for revenge.

All the time I had buried my tension and tried to avoid facing it, I suffered greater stress. It was only when I faced up to my memories and acknowledged my grief that I began to be healed. Now I saw that whenever I thought about the murderers who killed my family, I still wanted to punish them. The anger against them was as great as the grief for my family, and it burned inside me like a great ball of fire. I realised that I would never know true peace until I had dealt with this as well; I had to find a way of forgiving them, before the bitterness inside me destroyed me.

This was a difficult challenge. How could I ever forgive those who killed my family? Do I need to forget before I can forgive? What does forgiveness mean to me? I struggled with these questions, but in time I discovered that forgiveness opens a channel for real spiritual power to work in my life; a power which brings healing and wholeness.

First of all, does forgiving mean forgetting? I don't think so. By forgiving those who killed my family I haven't erased the painful experiences from my heart and memory: they will always remain. The images are always with me: the baby being clubbed and butchered; my father being knocked into the pit, his body slashed; the head of a younger brother axed into two pieces; the stomachs of another brother and sister torn out; my mother as she was dragged to be killed; Sopheak bound and hung on the fence like an animal, or Sophoan tied up to allow the mosquitoes to bite him for a whole night. And I have never forgotten the *chlop* who bludgeoned me from behind. The memories are always fresh. Sometimes, I wake up in the middle of the night feeling the absence of my family with new intensity. I miss them so much, it sometimes feels as though part of me has been amputated. I tried for years to forget the traumatic images of my family's death, but without success. The more I tried, the more vivid the images became. Finally I became aware that this was not the way to forgive: forgetting was impossible, and it wasn't the same as forgiving.

Once I asked some friends, "What does forgiveness mean?" They answered by telling me that I should "get in touch" with my bitterness. They said that if I didn't get in touch with it, I would never be able to forgive. I was furious: their words tore into me. I never asked them for that advice. They had never been in my shoes: what would they know about bitterness? What they knew was from their heads, not from experience or heart. They boxed my experience into their narrow frame and then tried to open a doorway to draw me out of their box. There I was, trying to understand the meaning of forgiveness, and they couldn't even see how much pain and hurt was in me. I knew the bitterness in my soul, and I'd had enough; I didn't need to get in touch with it.

When I first became a Christian, I realised that forgiveness was an important part of the Gospel, so I tried hard to find out about it. It hadn't been a feature of any religious teaching I'd known before. So I went to church and listened to the preachers: I always thought the messages were wonderful, but found myself struggling to apply them to my own life. One preacher taught about forgiveness from the parable of the prodigal son, and after his sermon I went up to him and asked, "What does it mean to forgive?" He looked at me and he stopped smiling. I thought he was going to give me an answer, but he only said, "Were you asleep while I was preaching?" I hadn't meant to offend him, but I felt terribly rejected. How was I ever going to understand?

Later I attended another service, where another preacher taught on the same subject, from the same story. Once again I went to him afterwards and asked him to explain more. He gave me his business card and said, "Give me a call sometime and we'll talk about it." I left that church wondering: did these preachers preach from their hearts or their heads? I'd listened to everything they said. They preached easily, but I wasn't sure it would be so easy for them to put their words into practice. If they'd experienced deep hurt themselves, they would have spoken from their hearts and shared their own battle with forgiveness. I wondered, "How would they feel if they were in my shoes?"

When I was young, my father used to tell me, "Don't take advantage of people by telling them to do something you yourself have never done. You have no idea how difficult it is." His words were reinforced when I spoke to the preachers: the school of preaching is easier than the school of practice. Forgiveness is very tough, and people who are hurt can't be taught to forgive just by saying, "Jesus said this and did that." A friend of mine tried to help me in that way: he opened the Bible and explained to me how Jesus forgave the offender. It was easy for him to teach me, but he didn't have to apply the teaching to deal with a terrible tragedy in his life like I did.

If you've been deeply hurt, it isn't easy to forgive. We can learn a lesson from Jesus, who forgave those who crucified him; we can learn from his parable of the prodigal son, that God is our loving Father who forgives us when we turn away from him. But we are only sinful human beings, and our journey to forgiveness is a long and hard one.

It's too easy to work out what the Bible says, and formulate it into a set of rules or teachings, and try to pass them on. Too many teachers and counsellors don't understand what pain has been suffered by the person they are helping, and they are afraid to get alongside and enter into the pain with that person. If they did, they might realise how intensely personal the problem of forgiveness is.

When I joined the police force, I turned down a chance to fulfil my first promise to my family and avenge their deaths. This refusal wasn't out of a spirit of forgiveness, but a simple choice: I chose not to kill to satisfy my anger. I had no idea at that time what forgiveness could mean. Later on, as I read the Bible and prayed, I began to realise that forgiveness begins with remembering and accepting the sinfulness of human beings. I had to accept what had happened in the past, but that was no easy task. So I was back at the old question: was it really necessary to forgive? The people who killed my family were evil, and they should be punished. Was it justice, to offer them forgiveness? Yet I needed to forgive them – not for their sake but for my own. As long as I was unable to forgive, that fire burned in my heart, and it was burning me down every day.

I knew that just as I dealt with my grief by facing up to the memories, I had to do the same with my rage and anger. Forgiving isn't pleasant: it means looking all these things in the face. I had to walk through all the trauma yet again, and acknowledge my true responses: the anger, the rage and the hatred I felt when the Khmer Rouge soldier pointed his gun at my head and ordered me to leave my bag or be shot dead; my helplessness when they tortured Sopheak and Sophoan; my anguish when they butchered my family and friends; my terror when they struck me from behind.

I listed everything I experienced and everything I felt, and this enabled me to see the reality of hatred and anger in my soul. I knew I had to dig it all out before I could fully forgive.

When I first began to pray about this, I asked the same question that Peter asked: "How many times do I forgive?" (Matthew 18:22,23). I was reluctant even to say "one" or "two" times, because I hadn't yet dealt with the hatred and bitterness in my heart. My refusal to forgive meant that I never gained internal peace, and that ball of fire continued to consume me. I held on to the pictures of my tormentors: I saw their faces in my mind's eye, and whenever I thought of them I would be filled with the same helpless rage I had felt as a small boy. I wanted to cut them into small pieces, crush them and kill them. I wanted them to feel the pain I went through, to cry as I had cried. I wanted them to tell me how they felt as pain was inflicted on them. I dwelt on these thoughts and couldn't escape from them. Yet logic told me that even if I could kill hundreds of them, my heart wouldn't be satisfied. Even if I could bomb a whole village of those who killed my family, it wouldn't be enough.

> Do not repay anyone evil for evil. Be careful to do what is right in the eyes of everybody. If it is possible, as far as it depends on you, live at peace with everyone. Do not take revenge, my friends, but leave room for God's wrath, for it is written: 'It is mine to avenge; I will repay,' says the Lord. (Romans 12:17–19)

The apostle Paul is right: I shouldn't repay evil for evil: it's none of my business. Forgiveness doesn't come through vengeance, and neither does forgetting: no amount of violence could erase my memories. So I gave up my urge to inflict pain on those who had hurt me and killed my family. I knew it wouldn't help, and nursing those desires was only damaging me – my emotional, spiritual, physical and psychological being. Hebrews 12:15 warns, "See to it . . . that no bitter root grows up to cause trouble and defile many." I know the consequences of that root of bitterness. I had to make a deliberate effort to pull it out from my heart and soul.

As I gave up my desire for revenge, and pulled out the root of hatred, anger and bitterness from my heart, I was journeying towards forgiveness, and the healing of my soul and the wiping away of its tears. Doing this required putting my will power ahead of some very powerful emotions. I realised that I had to make the decision to forgive those who killed my family. Since God had forgiven me, it was right for me to forgive them, even though it seemed impossible to do so. So I prayed:

> Lord God, I have tasted enough bitterness in my life. The pictures of the killers are in my mind every day, and I have no peace but only hatred, anger and bitterness in my heart and soul. The fire of my anger burns in my heart, and it's destroying me. I can only make the decision to forgive. Father God, I ask you to grant me power to put out the fire that has been there for years. Grant me peace and clean my heart as I forgive those who killed my family.

Forgiveness has been a special gift from God in my life. It's a spiritual power, breaking the tie which bound the images of the killers in my soul. It cleaned away the bitterness from my heart. As I learned that God forgives my mistakes, and that a forgiving attitude is essential for well-being, I experienced healing in my soul. Forgiveness is indeed holy medicine from God, which I needed badly. It was true that I couldn't do this for myself, like the knife in the Cambodian saying. I needed a power outside myself, and that power was the love of God.

Since I have forgiven those who killed my family, my life has changed. The fire of hatred has gone from my heart and soul, though the bitterness has not been forgotten. By forgiving completely, I can move ahead, relying on God's healing power. Forgiveness has released me from the emotional torment that burned within me for years, and now my heart is lighter and my spirit has peace.

CHAPTER NINE

WHY PAIN?

"For just as the sufferings of Christ flow over into our lives, so also through Christ our comfort overflows."
(2 Corinthians 1:5)

Ever since I lost my family during the brutal Khmer Rouge Communist regime, I have been trying to find hope, and searching for the meaning of pain and suffering. My struggles led me to find new hope in Jesus: he has given me the courage and strength to walk through the fire of pain. Without hope from Jesus, I would never have been able to put the broken pieces of my life back together.

For us, living in a broken world, it's hard to find an answer to the question of pain, yet we know that suffering is everywhere; it is the texture of the human condition. The universal fact of suffering raises profound questions about the worth of life, questions that can't be avoided. I don't intend to teach about this here, but merely to highlight some experiences of suffering and some thoughts about the problem of evil. Thinking about the nature of evil cannot be avoided if we are thinking about the problem of pain, for the two seem to be inextricably linked. No one who has suffered would suggest that suffering is a good thing – yet I can't say that it is wholly bad. Painful though my experiences have been, they have made me a stronger person, better able to understand the reality of life.

Suffering has many dimensions, and perhaps the most common is physical pain: everyone has suffered it at some time, in varying degrees. It can be constructive: a useful warning that something is wrong, or that some of our habits are unhealthy; it gives us a chance to correct things. Athletes speak of going through the pain barrier when they are pushing their bodies to achieve success on the track or field. They say, "No pain, no gain", and accept that pain is a price they are willing to pay for their fitness. It has a purpose.

A different kind of pain is the emotional and spiritual anguish suffered by all of us when we lose a loved one. Bereavement disrupts the whole structure of our lives and throws us into chaos. It can feel similar to physical pain and indeed can cause it. (My own experiences with Post-Traumatic Stress Disorder showed me that analgesics may relieve the symptoms but cannot remove the cause.) Yet every relationship carries the possibility of pain: to risk loving someone is to risk the pain of losing them. Even our most casual relationships can bring with them misunderstandings; the making of difficult decisions; having to face the pressures of growing up, making a living, coping with family, friends and marriages. All can cause us pain in the everyday mixture of happiness and sadness which is daily life. Living hurts.

Some people seek to escape pain through pleasure, the abuse of alcohol or drugs; some are driven to despair and suicide. Some seek solace in religion while others blame God for their troubles and reject it all. Yet the experience of pain always has some positive aspects: it can increase our compassion for others, and our understanding of what other people may be feeling, even when their experience is different from our own.

At first my understanding of my experiences was coloured by growing up in a Buddhist society. Buddhist philosophy indicates that suffering is everywhere. Gautama's enlightenment experience consisted of discovering four truths about suffering: that it is universal; that it is caused by the selfish desire for a separate, individual existence; that it ceases when human passions are extinguished and the selfish embrace of life has been renounced; and that only following the true Buddhist path leads to peace and the end of suffering. The philosophy of karma extends this. Khmer Buddhist society views karma as both actions and their consequences: you reap what you sow. Any selfish act will cause suffering, either in this life or in your next incarnation. So if you are suffering in your life today, it is your own fault. You must have committed bad deeds in a previous life. When I was an adolescent, trying to deal with the pain of all that happened to me during those years, this doctrine dealt me yet another blow: it judged me and blamed me for my own misery.

It was in the darkness of this utter despair that the message of Christ dawned in my heart and gave me the first glimmering of the hope that was to transform my life. Christianity doesn't point a finger at the sufferer and tell him that everything is his own fault; it says, instead, that suffering is part of a much bigger picture. The Bible teaches that the whole of creation is fallen from its original perfect state, and the evil we observe is part of that fallen condition. This is a complex theology, but even though I understood it only partially, the joy of that great truth broke in on me: I wasn't responsible for what happened to me. There was evil in the hearts of men, and it had emerged to pursue a political end which destroyed millions of innocent people, my family included. Other men had been swept up in Pol Pot's madness and evil, and had joined in by committing atrocities. I had suffered physical pain, psychological torture and emotional anguish, but it had been the result of someone else's evil actions, not my own. This released me from a terrible bondage that had hampered my recovery for years.

Of course, logic goes on to ask difficult questions: if God is both good and all-powerful, how can evil exist? Either he is good (in which case he does not have the power to destroy evil), or he has the power (in which case he chooses to allow evil, and cannot be good). This debate has raged for centuries among theologians; one view is that God chooses to give us free will, so that we can choose for ourselves between good and evil, just as Adam in the Garden of Eden chose to eat the fruit of the knowledge of good and evil, and opened the way for evil to enter the world.

Certainly there is no doubt that evil permeates our world. We are plagued with greed, jealousy and a desire for power, which leads in turn to injustice, exploitation, racial and cultural prejudice, and wars. On an intimate level, personal relationships degenerate into selfish struggles for power, so that friendships and marriages break down. On a societal level, economic differences widen, as sections of society grab what they can for themselves with no compassion for the struggles of others. Internationally, countries behave in the same way, seeking to dominate and oppress others. Technology is misused, so the environment becomes polluted and weapons become ever more destructive. At the time of writing, the terrorist attack on the World Trade Center in the United States on 11th September 2001 has provoked a "war on terrorism" which seems doomed to escalate. We can't see into the future, but it's certain that many more people will suffer. We are free to choose our own morality, free to seek God or turn away from him, and every day we make that choice. "Justice is far from us, and righteousness does not reach us." (Isaiah 59:9)

Sometimes it seems as though history repeats itself over and over again: Adolf Hitler tried to exterminate the Jews and establish a society of his own design, excluding one particular race; the "Gang of Four" who led the Cultural Revolution in China were responsible for destroying particular groups of intellectuals who might oppose their regime; Pol Pot in Cambodia intended to cancel all previous history and begin at Year Zero, exterminating millions of his own countrymen in the process.

Why does God allow all this to happen? The fact is that our logical questions don't help us, any more than the deliberations of his friends helped Job. The Book of Job is an amazing guide to the problem of suffering and pain. Job is a blameless, prosperous and upright man, who holds God in reverence and opposes all wrongdoing. Yet God allows him to be tested by Satan, with the loss of all he holds dear. When Job's friends come to comfort him, they see the extent of his pain and fall silent. Then Job speaks: his words are not addressed to his friends; they are barely addressed to God. In fact, it is a bitter cry for death, which alone seems to offer him hope of comfort and rest. The friends debate the issues and offer answers which seem to have some theological content, but they fail to satisfy Job.

Once when I was doing my graduate studies, I shared my story with a group of friends, and tried to tell them something of what had happened to me and the long-lasting effects it had. When I had finished, one of them said, "I know how you feel . . ." His words struck me an icy blow. There was no way they could "know" how I felt. Theirs was a purely intellectual understanding. The same man went on, "What do you want from us?" as if I was expecting them to help me. That wasn't so – all I needed was someone to sit patiently with me and feel with me. They were always looking for solutions, as though there was a magic formula to do away with my pain. I knew from bitter experience that there was no simple answer – if there were, I would have found it. I had been searching urgently enough. They tried all the current psychological tricks: suggesting that I should "get in touch" with my bitterness, and that I was "running away from my pain". They suggested that I should get angry with God – yet I knew in my heart that God didn't kill my family, so I couldn't blame him. They were very much like Job's friends.

Ultimately, the only answer is the one that God gives in the final chapters of the book: that God is there, and that in his power he is watching over Job. This may not have made sense to Job's friends, but in the New Testament we are given a new understanding of God – as one who stands beside us in his Son and shares our experience of pain.

Jesus came to the world to demonstrate his love on the cross. When we receive him as Lord of our lives he gives us hope, love and eternal life, but he doesn't guarantee that we will have freedom from pain. For me, the cross is a symbol of pain, a trophy which signifies Christ's glorious victory over suffering and death. We can share in that victory, but our Christian life will also give us a share of the pain. Peter encourages us, "Dear friends, do not be surprised at the painful trial you are suffering, as though something strange were happening to you. But rejoice that you participate in the sufferings of Christ, so that you may be overjoyed when his glory is revealed." (I Peter 4:12–13).

A few years ago, a friend who was not a Christian challenged me, "If the cross is a trophy of pain, why do you want to be a Christian? Why do you want to live in pain?" I could not think how to answer him at first; it was so clear that he didn't understand what following Christ meant. Then I looked at the apple I was eating and asked him, "What does this apple taste like? Sweet or sour?"

"Don't be ridiculous," he replied. "How can I know that? I'm not the one who's eating it!"

"That's right," I answered. "And you can't know what the Christian life means if you haven't accepted Jesus for yourself. You don't know how it feels if you haven't shared in Jesus' love and his pain."

We trust that God never forsakes us, and that his fatherly love is with us all the time. This is what transforms the experience of suffering, for the principle of love was shown to us by the supreme example of Jesus. No one in this world has demonstrated love and care for us like Jesus: God's one and only Son humbled himself by dying on the cross for our sins.

When we accept that we are loved by the love made visible at the cross of Christ, then we begin to understand the nature of God. We also begin to understand the principle of love, that sacrifices self for another's good.

As the Father has loved me, so have I loved you. Now remain in my love. If you obey my commands, you will remain in my love, just as I have obeyed my Father's commands and remain in his love. I have told you this so that my joy may be in you and that your joy may be complete. My command is this: love each other as I have loved you. Greater love has no one than this, that he lay down his life for his friends. (John 15:9–13)

Here we touch one of the secrets of the universe, and possibly part of the answer to the problem of pain. When the principle of love has taken root in our hearts and souls, we may stop killing each other, hurting each other, cheating each other, abusing each other. Just as Buddhism places the cause of pain squarely in the court of the self, and the selfish pursuit of one's own interests, so the sacrifice of selfish desires through the principle of love can offer the solution.

> Love is patient, love is kind. It does not envy, it does not boast, it is not proud. It is not rude, it is not self-seeking, it is not easily angered, it keeps no record of wrongs. Love does not delight in evil but rejoices with the truth. It always protects, always trusts, always hopes, always perseveres. Love never fails. (1 Corinthians 13:4–8)

Love drives us towards others with no expectation of reward; it fundamentally alters our lives. If love has profoundly taken root in our hearts and souls, it will surely reduce suffering as we reach out to others and consider their welfare before our own. It gives us a vision of a world very different from the one we live in: a glimpse of the kingdom of heaven.

This is why love gives us hope and a reason for living, a deep trust in the good purposes of God. Some people's hopes are for the future, ambitions for careers or lifestyle. The Christian's hope is more profound: a trust that whatever befalls us in this life, and whatever sufferings we endure, Jesus is beside us, suffering with us, and leading us on to follow in his footsteps and live in his way.

> We . . . rejoice in our sufferings, because we know that suffering produces perseverance; perseverance, character; and character, hope. And hope does not disappoint us, because God has poured out his love into our hearts by the Holy Spirit, whom he has given us. (Romans 5:3–5)

Only those who have passed through deep pain know how to come alongside those who are in pain. In the last year of my graduate studies, I experienced chronic pain in my left side. What was wrong with me? If I lay down to sleep, the pain attacked me: I couldn't sleep and I couldn't sit in the classroom; all I could do was to stand, for the whole day. I went to see several doctors who conducted tests, but they couldn't find anything wrong with me. The problem went on for months.

In the middle of all this I received a card from Sharon, the wife of a professor. It said, "Reaksa, the words on the other side of this card comforted me when I was going through a difficult time. My sister gave them to me because the same words ministered to her when she was battling with cancer a few years ago." On the other side were words that comforted my heart deeply:

> There is a Power beyond our power,
> A hand that clasps our hand,
> There is a strength beyond our strength,
> A heart that understands.
> There is a smile that warms our souls,
> A calm, assuring peace.
> And at the mercy seat of God
> There's grace that cannot cease.
> So in your weary, trying days
> May it comfort you to know
> The Father guards your life with love
> And never leaves his own.
>
> Judith Gooding

I was grateful because this was clearly someone who knew what pain was like. Her soul connected with mine because she sought to understand my suffering. Sharon often telephoned to see how I was doing, and her calls always encouraged me. She always told me, "We've been praying for you every day, Reaksa. We hope you'll be better soon."

After all the doctors had failed to find an illness, I came to my own conclusions: I was still suffering from emotional pain. Earlier that year, I'd made the decision to write this book. I'd tried to start writing, but I always gave up after a few lines. It was when I nerved myself to begin writing, reliving those years in the jungle, that the physical symptoms began. I understand much more about psychosomatic pain now: as soon as I had completed the first draft and given it to others to read, I was able to relax and began to feel better. When it was returned to me and I started working on it again, the pain returned. Whenever I sat down to write I found myself weeping, but now I wasn't ashamed. I was releasing the pain in my soul, and the more I cried, the healthier I became. I knew it wasn't a sign of weakness or lack of character, but it was the art of easing pain.

Writing the book confronted me with all the old problems that plagued me: Why did all this happen to me? Why did my family have to die? In other words, why should the innocent suffer? Round I went again on the theological, logical merry-go-round. Even though I had become a Christian, I was still wrestling with the questions. I wanted to ask God, but I didn't hear any answers, until I realised the truth. Where was God in my suffering? He was beside me, suffering with me, crying with me. Jesus became a man so that he could know the depths of human suffering, abandonment, loneliness and physical pain, right up to death and beyond. Only those who have known deep pain themselves can come alongside those who suffer: now I realised that God himself understands the pain. In fact he knows the path of pain intimately, because he once walked through it – for us.

Racked with pain beyond tears, the kind of pain which no one else seemed to know, I badly needed to sense God's presence, and to feel his love, more than anything else. God didn't magically take away my pain, but he gave me hope so that I could walk through it. It wasn't a hope that I would forget what had happened to me (how could I forget my loved ones?) but the hope that comes from a new life in Christ. It was the presence of the Holy Spirit walking with me through the fire, and showing me that God had a purpose and a challenge for the rest of my life with him.

When Jesus was about to face the cross, he comforted his disciples by telling them this:

> I tell you the truth, you will weep and mourn while the world rejoices. You will grieve, but your grief will turn to joy. A woman giving birth to a child has pain because her time has come; but when her baby is born she forgets the anguish because of her joy that a child is born into the world. So with you: Now is your time of grief, but I will see you again and you will rejoice, and no one will take away your joy. (John 16:20–22)

When we are able to walk through the pain, we too will rejoice. It has been more than twenty-five years since I lost my family, and now I can see meaning in what I have endured. By the grace of God, I walked through the pain, and like a woman's pain in childbirth giving way to joy in the new birth, I have found life. It gave me the courage to share my story with all those who live on after the loss of their loved ones. I also have the courage to pick up every broken piece of my life, rebuilding it through my hope in Jesus Christ. After the valley of tears and pain, I have found the joy of life through the promise of God: "Those who sow in tears will reap with songs of joy. He who goes out weeping, carrying seed to sow, will return with songs of joy, carrying sheaves with him." (Psalm 126:5–6)

The journey of pain continues, but I am not discouraged because I have someone special who is walking with me and who knows my path. He is my ultimate hope.

It is well with my soul,
It is well with my soul,
It is well, it is well with my soul.

CHAPTER TEN

RETURNING HOME

"He who dares to face the fears, knows how to heal the fears."

When I boarded the plane at Bangkok on 14th May 1989 I said farewell to Cambodia for ever. I never intended to return to my homeland again: it held too many bitter memories for me. I settled in Canada and built a new life for myself, and although I spent a great deal of time coming to terms with the shattering events of my early life, I considered that it was all behind me. I thought of Cambodia a great deal, because for many years I was tormented by my vivid memories, but they were just that – memories. My sister Sopheap was still living just outside Siemreap city, and I exchanged letters with her perhaps once or twice a year, yet I managed never to think of Cambodia as a real place, which had changed and moved on as I had. I never thought of it as a place I might visit.

While I was engaged in my studies at Providence Theological Seminary, friends often asked me if I had ever thought about returning to serve the Lord in Cambodia; I always replied in the same way: "I'm never going back." What on earth would be the point of going back to the place where

I lost everything? I had run away from there, and I'd found a place of peace, freedom and new life. Why go back to a place where memories could rise up and assail me all over again, where fighting might break out at any time? I didn't even consider it. Yet as I grew in my Christian life, I often prayed that God would show me the direction he wanted my life to take.

When I graduated in 1996 I considered that I'd finally completed my formal education, which had been so disrupted in my youth, and I set myself to earn my living. I decided to set up my own cleaning business: throughout my college career I'd supported myself by working for a local cleaning firm, so I had a good idea of how such a service operated. Some of my friends thought this was a strange occupation for someone with a master's degree but I didn't care: I was working hard and it was a challenge. Business was slow for the first year or so, though I earned enough to keep myself; then it really got off the ground and I took on more employees to help me. I had about a hundred regular customers.

Life in Canada was good to me: I had a home, friends, a church, and a good income from my own business. I felt settled. Then, late in 1998, I received a disturbing email from Dr Duc Nguyen, of World Vision USA, based in California. The church in Cambodia was close to his heart, and he was deeply concerned for the Christians there. The church had grown slowly since the first evangelical missionaries had visited the country in 1923, but in the 1970s the seeds sown in those early days suddenly began to bear fruit. In the years of war before the country fell to the Communists, the Bible School in Phnom Penh was swamped with people eager to hear the Good News of Jesus. The fruit of its labours was soon evident: in 1970 there were some 300 Christians in the city; in 1975, when the school was closed by the Khmer Rouge, there were 3,000. What those Christians suffered, along with their fellow countrymen, no one will ever know, but a remnant was left when the evacuations and killing finally ended. I had come upon a thriving church in Khao I Dang refugee camp, and some of those people had faithfully made their way back to serve their people in Phnom Penh as soon as they could. The Bible School had finally reopened in 1992.

Dr Nguyen told me that the school was now in desperate need of teachers, and challenged me to return to Cambodia to teach there. I spoke the language, I understood the culture, and I had the benefit of my biblical studies in Canada: I was the ideal candidate. I didn't even consider the proposition. I replied politely but firmly, "I'm not interested."

However, for days after I'd sent my refusal, I couldn't stop thinking about it. I knew I didn't want to return, but why was I so set against it? I rationalised my decision by saying that I had a business to run, and employees who depended on me; it would be hard to leave. Yet I knew there was more to it than that. I recognised the sensations of unease which that email had aroused in me: I was still afraid. I was afraid of my own memories, and I was afraid of facing up to the reality of what had happened in my country. I knew that if I returned, I would meet people who were as hurt and damaged by those years as I had been. How could a country move into the future when most of its population had been involved in such bloodshed?

I took my concerns to a trusted friend who had been a missionary in South Africa, and her reply was unhesitating. "I can appreciate your concerns, Reaksa," she said. "But you're the right person to do this work. It's a wonderful opportunity to serve the Lord." I listened to her, because I knew she was a faithful Christian, but I was very quiet: this wasn't really the advice I wanted to hear. She looked at me shrewdly: "Are you really seeking the will of God, or is your mind made up already?" Her question struck me to the heart.

When I got home, I got on my knees for some serious prayer time. I needed to ask for direction from the Lord, but I needed also to ask myself some hard questions. Was I seriously seeking the will of God? Was I really living for Christ or for myself? I realised I didn't know the answers, and I needed to examine my own heart. It took me months of prayer to work my way towards the truth.

It was during this period that I had an accident; I fell and injured my back while stripping a floor. It was totally incapacitating: I couldn't bend, I couldn't push or pull a cleaning machine, and even driving a car was very painful. I went to see back specialists, but they all said that there wasn't anything to be done: all I could do was to be careful and avoid lifting heavy objects. In a business which depends on operating heavy cleaning machinery this was bad news. I tried chiropractors and Chinese traditional therapists, but there was no improvement.

This wasn't like any of the times I had been ill before: this wasn't any kind of psychosomatic pain. There was a clear cause and effect: I had a fall and I hurt my back. It was simple and straightforward and yet there was apparently no simple cure. My life was totally disrupted, and it was at this point that I saw God's hand at work. My last excuse had gone: I couldn't work at my cleaning business any longer. I had nothing to stop me from serving him in Cambodia.

I knew that my refusal to consider the proposal lay in my fears, and I had to face up to them, so I started seeking advice from many Christian friends. I called Dr Nguyen several times, and he always encouraged me. "It's not so much what you've learned," he said. "The most important thing is how you digest what you've learned." I spoke to Bishop David Cochran, who had helped me through my graduate studies. He had more than twenty years' experience of helping immigrant Cambodians to settle into the USA, and he, too, told me that I was the right person to do this work. Even my friend Margaret, from Downview Northminster Baptist Church, supported me. She was a specially precious friend because she never proffered advice, but she often prayed with me and helped me to seek the will of God honestly and with confidence.

Finally, I was ready to accept God's call. I went to see Brian Stiller, President of Tyndale College and Seminary, and told him of my decision. He said, "Well, Reaksa, this is what you've been training for: you have to go and preach the Good News. I know you'll be a good messenger to your people." We prayed together, and when I left, he hugged me and said, "May God's blessing be with you."

My foster mother was also a part of my decision-making; although we live far apart physically, we're very close emotionally, and she shared my mixed feelings about returning. She was happy to know that I was actively seeking God's will for my life, and that I was preparing to serve him in Cambodia. She was also excited that I'd be able to meet up with Sopheap, my only surviving sister. But she knew how bad things had been, and she knew that it wouldn't be easy for me to go back to Cambodia. Mom knew what was in my heart.

Even though my mind was made up, I didn't know what the future held. I didn't know if I would actually be able to complete the task I'd set myself, so I thought I'd better take things one step at a time. I handed over the cleaning business to my friend Chann Vanh, who worked for me, and told him to keep things going. If I returned to Canada in the next few months, I'd come back and work in the business again. It was a kind of safety net: if it turned out that I couldn't handle things in Cambodia, I'd be able to take up my old life in Canada where I left off.

On 20th May 1999 I set out for the airport in Toronto, dropping off a note on my way to say goodbye to Mom. Lots of friends came to see me off, and as we stood in the departure lounge they gathered around to pray for me. I was strengthened by their loving support, and by the renewed sense that we were brothers and sisters in Christ; I was not going back to Cambodia alone.

As the plane lifted off, I could think only of my homeland – the land that had inflicted both physical and psychological scars and given me unforgettable memories of pain. I had never forgotten the three promises I made in front of my family's grave: to take revenge, to dedicate myself as a Buddhist monk, or to leave Cambodia for ever. At the time I was seriously determined to fulfil those promises, but I had broken them, one after another: I had never taken revenge; I had not even remained a Buddhist; and although I had indeed left the country, here I was, on my way back. The trip was filled with mixed emotions, the memories of childhood fears, of adult bitterness, and of the long road I had trodden on my way to recovery.

Sometimes recovery seemed like a never-ending process; just when I thought I had conquered one fear, another would crop up, and make me feel helpless and inadequate all over again. I knew I trusted God; I knew that my hope in Jesus had brought me healing and peace, and I wanted to share that peace with my people, who had suffered as I had. Would I be able to do it? Or would the sights and sounds of my homeland take me back to being the shaken, suffering child I had been then?

I was nervous about how I would manage. My studies in mission and cultural communication had taught me how important it was to acclimatise myself back into my original culture. If I was to be able to communicate with people, I had to be able to see things from their point of view. But I had been away for fifteen years, and there must have been a lot of changes in society. How much did I really know about my country today? Even though I pretended to myself that I was not worried, I kept praying all the time.

The flight took over twenty hours, and I was tired when we touched down at Pochentong Airport, just outside Phnom Penh. I collected my bags and joined the queue of people waiting to apply for a visa. When it was my turn, I handed my passport and application form to the policeman behind the counter. He took them, flipped through the pages and looked up at me.

"Are you Khmer?" he asked.

"Yes," I responded in Khmer.

"Where were you born?"

"In Siemreap," I answered.

"What are you doing here?"

"Visiting my relatives."

He looked back at my form, wrote something on it, and put it underneath a pile of other documents. He turned round and spoke to another policeman standing behind him, then turned to the man behind me in the queue, took his passport, stamped it and returned it. I was left standing at the head of the queue, totally ignored. I couldn't believe what was happening. Then another policeman came up beside me and said in a low voice, "If you want to get it done quickly, I can help you. Just give me as much as you want; it's up to you."

For a moment I was so shocked, I didn't know what to say or think. I hadn't been in the country for twenty minutes, and already I was out of my depth. I had been a policeman myself once, and not a very good one, but I'd never asked for bribes. I couldn't believe that corruption had become so widespread.

When I looked around the airport, I realised that I could see several other policemen, all trying similar tactics to get money from the incoming passengers.

I didn't answer the policeman who'd asked me for money, but turned back to the official behind the counter.

"Sir, can you tell me what's wrong with my form and passport, please?"

He looked up at me and asked, "Where are they?"

"Under there. I saw you put them down." He lifted a few documents up, then turned away to do something else. I was very annoyed, but I was also aware of a rising unease. Not far away a woman was having a strident argument in Khmer with another official. She kept shouting that he had taken her passport, and he kept denying that he had it. "I've been here for an hour," she was saying. "You must give it back to me." I didn't know exactly what was going on, but I could guess: she was going to have to hand over some cash in order to get it back. I didn't want to fall into the same trap, but I didn't want to be held up indefinitely. It would be very inconvenient if I lost my passport.

I turned back to the other policeman. "I'll give you $5 if you can get my visa done quickly," I offered.

"That's not enough, *bong*," he replied. "I have many associates. Give me $10."

I could hardly believe my ears. Not content with taking bribes, they were bargaining, too! I kept thinking that if this happened in Canada, they would all lose their jobs. I didn't want to get involved with this corrupt business, but I couldn't see how I was going to get out of the airport otherwise. I handed over my ten dollars, he signalled to another official, and five minutes later I had my passport and visa safely in my hand and was walking out of the airport. I had come home, and found that it was a foreign country.

Once outside, I recognised Mr Say Bunthan, the administrator of Phnom Penh Bible School, whom I'd met five years earlier at a conference in the USA. He greeted me warmly and introduced me to Dr Andrew Kwong, the Academic Dean. Dr Kwong was a Chinese medical missionary from Hong Kong who went to help Cambodians fleeing along the Thai-Cambodian border almost twenty years before.

The street outside was busy: as we put my luggage into Dr Kwong's car, we were surrounded by people leaving the airport, rushing into the arms of relatives and friends, sometimes hugging and crying with joy. I wished for a moment that I had a family to welcome me like that. Sopheap didn't know I was back in Cambodia, and I hadn't written to her for a while. Now, as I stood in Phnom Penh, I realised that she was less than 300 miles away in Pouk district, and I longed to visit her.

As Dr Kwong drove me through the city, I was shocked. Everything had changed, and I couldn't recognise any landmarks at all. I could see that the standard of living had improved enormously: there were shops and hotels, the houses looked better built and the people better dressed. And there were so many cars! But the traffic system seemed completely out of control – we saw four minor accidents on that journey alone. How could the Cambodians drive so recklessly? Even the busiest road in Canada was a model of calm organisation by comparison. Once again I found myself judging my native country by the standards of my adopted one; I felt like a foreigner, and I wondered again if I was really able to do the job I had come to do.

Once I was settled, the Bible School gave me my teaching schedule: term began in September, and so I had three months free, to acclimatise and get to know Cambodia again. I decided it was time to visit my sister Sopheap.

From Phnom Penh to Siemreap took about six hours by boat; in late May the water level in Tonle Sap lake was very low, and only small boats could navigate it safely. On the way I thought about how I was going to find my sister; I wasn't sure I could find her house alone. I also knew that it probably wasn't safe for me to make my way to Pouk district, ten miles outside the city. I was wearing my Canadian clothes, and I looked wealthy by local standards: I could easily be mugged or kidnapped. I went instead to my friend Srun, and stayed in his house while he went to collect Sopheap.

Sopheap didn't believe Srun at first when he told her that I'd asked him to pick her up.

"Who's Reaksa?" she asked.

"You know, your brother from Canada," he replied.

"Are you sure? How can he be here?" she kept saying. "He left a long time ago. He never said he was coming back."

Eventually he persuaded her, and she and her daughter jumped hurriedly into his car and sped back to meet me.

It was a wonderful reunion. We held each other tightly, and Sopheap wouldn't let me go. She kept saying, "Reaksa! I've missed you so much! I just want to hold on to you! I can't believe you've come back to us!"

That first night we talked till three in the morning, just catching up on the last fifteen years. We talked about the family, our childhood, all our shared memories. She asked me about Canada and told me about her life in Cambodia. We had a lot to talk about.

Not all my encounters were as happy. I sought out my other relatives who had survived the killing fields, but in many cases we didn't recognise each other: we had all changed too much. We would begin to talk and piece together the missing years for all of us, but as soon as they discovered I had become a Christian, they grew angry with me. They felt I had betrayed my family as well as the Buddhist culture, because I wouldn't perform the usual religious rites to show respect to my parents. When my aunt's husband died, the situation grew worse. At the funeral I was expected to kneel before a statue of Buddha and before my uncle's coffin. It was a big spiritual dilemma – if I refused to kneel and perform the rites I would be cast out of the family, but if I knelt to worship Buddha I would violate my faith in God. My cousins pressed me to give in, but I told them I had to follow my own path to God. I had to remain faithful to Christ, who had rescued me from years of despair. I tried to tell my aunt how I felt, but she didn't say a word, and wouldn't even look at me. It was hard for me to resist their pleas. For years I had longed to have a family to love and accept me as one of them, and now I had been reunited with some of my relatives, I was being rejected by them. To my surprise, I found I understood their feelings; they had a right to be angry, and I was strong enough to cope with their anger.

While I was staying in Siemreap I was able to spend a month as a volunteer at the mental health hospital, where I saw patients every day. There I began to learn how Cambodians were handling the emotional and psychological traumas inflicted by the years of conflict and the repression of their culture. There are millions of people suffering from these conditions, but no psychologists, counsellors or psychiatrists with enough knowledge of mental health to help their own people. I worked alongside doctors to diagnose and counsel many patients suffering from depression, and I also taught them progressive relaxation techniques. It was a wonderful feeling to be helping my own people, and at last I felt that my harrowing experiences were being put to some use.

After my stint at the hospital, I returned to Phnom Penh to the Bible School in time for the dedication ceremony held in

October 1999. I felt privileged to be present on such an historic occasion: it was attended by the government minister for Religions and Cults, who gave us the freedom to proclaim the Good News. His support for Christianity is very important, and persuaded me that God is doing miraculous work in Cambodia.

I enjoyed working in the school. To me, to teach is to learn, and I learned that perhaps the greatest need in Cambodia is for counselling. Most of my students carried unresolved emotional issues, a legacy from their parents and the past, though many of them are scarcely aware of their own problems. It saddens me to see another generation of my own people suffering second hand from the trauma of the Khmer Rouge period.

Outside my working hours I spent time talking to people about their lives. Twenty years after the end of the Khmer Rouge regime, their experiences during that time still represented their most important, vivid, long-lasting memories. All the people I talked to had lost at least one member of their family, sometimes in horrific circumstances, and this legacy of loss has never been dealt with properly. So at the end of my first year at the Bible School, I suggested to Dr Kwong that I should teach a counselling course. He agreed readily, because he understood how deep the needs were, and he felt that such a course could offer a real hope of healing for many people.

The course was designed not for the ordinary students, but for pastors and church leaders. The aim was to help them look first at their own problems and unresolved grief, and then to enable them to turn outward and become aware of the needs in their congregations. When they were able to offer help to the many troubled people with whom they came into contact, they would be able to start a healing process that could spread across the land.

Teaching the course wasn't easy, because Cambodian culture doesn't allow people to talk about their emotions. Psychological problems are a cause of shame, so they are never talked about outside the family. Distress, grief and pain are usually buried deeply; the sufferer assumes a public mask and refuses to discuss them. As a result, problems go untreated, because any medical diagnosis of mental illness would bring intense humiliation.

All my counselling students had lived through the Khmer Rouge regime, and all had lost relatives and suffered deep wounds. Unresolved grief was a major problem in their lives, often appearing as psychological and physical symptoms, yet they were initially very reluctant to open up these old wounds. They refused to get in touch with their feelings, hiding behind the defensive walls they had built up over the years. It took almost the whole year to begin to break through; in the process, I encountered all their denials, resistance, anger, frustrations and fears. It was a difficult task, but God gave me a spirit of patience and wisdom to work through it with them. He also gave me the courage to share my own experiences, not just of pain but of recovery. Now they are able to recognise their defence mechanisms, and understand that it takes courage to break down the walls they've been hiding behind, to come out and live freely in the love of Jesus Christ. Healing will take time, but we trust in the power of the Holy Spirit to make it complete.

Despite all the difficulties, I have found great joy in serving the Lord in my homeland and helping my own people. I have planted churches in my home town to spread the Good News of Jesus Christ, and I have taught other church leaders to spread the gospel of healing. I've given seminars on psychological trauma, and I plan others on anger and forgiveness, so that I can share what I have learned so painfully.

After I lost my family, I thought I could never be happy again, because my pain and fear prevented me from experiencing joy and happiness. Now all that hurt has been turned into joy, as I find that God has a special purpose for my life. Cambodians have suffered a great deal. Only the healing message of hope, love and forgiveness from Jesus Christ can make them whole again – as I have been made whole.

Jesus said, "If anyone would come after me, he must deny himself and take up his cross and follow me. For whoever wants to save his life will lose it, but whoever loses his life for me will find it." (Matthew 16:24–25)

POSTSCRIPT

I remember the first day I arrived back in Cambodia. Dr Andrew Kwong, the Dean of Phnom Penh Bible School (PPBS) took me for lunch at a Chinese restaurant. He asked me, "Reaksa, would you like to marry a local girl?" I quickly replied, "I do not see that happening." He asked me, "Why not?" I did not know what to answer. At that time, I was not sure how I would want to settle down. In my heart, I knew that I longed to have a family of my own to replace the one that I had lost two decades earlier. But in some respects I felt pulled between two cultures. Could I marry a local girl?

Surprisingly, God changed my life, and six months after my arrival I met Sophaly Eng. She was not a Christian then. I invited her for lunch, but I was not interested in pursuing a relationship because my priority was to find a *Christian* girl. However, I did speak to her about Jesus Christ. She did not say anything, but asked several questions about Christianity. I shared more with her and invited her to come to my church.

One day, Sophaly approached Pastor Bunthan, and asked him more about the Christian faith. The Pastor spent some time telling her about Christ, and two months later she accepted Jesus Christ as her personal Lord and Saviour. On 11th November 2000, Sophaly and I were married in Phnom Penh. Our son, Philos Reaksa Himm was born on 15th July 2002 in Toronto, Canada. Sophaly and Philos have brought great joy to my heart.

By the middle of 2002, I decided to leave my job at the Bible School so that I could live near my hometown of Pouk. I wanted to do church planting work and to mentor the local leaders. Actually, it took me 13 years to pray about returning to my hometown. It brought back many sad memories, and I was rejected by my own people. Despite this, I chose to accept them and tried to get to know them better. Now, we have established three small house-churches in local villages, and by the grace of God, we will plant churches in more villages.

In April 2003 my family and I travelled to the UK, with the help of SAO Cambodia, for the launch of this book. Questions from those who came to hear my story prompted me to seek face-to-face reconciliation with my family's killers. This was not easy and I needed much prayer from friends around the world. Then on 6th June 2003, I went back to the village where my family was killed. I discovered that four of the six men involved had been killed and one had moved to a different village. I met the remaining one. He was fearful of meeting me but I spoke to him of God's love and forgiveness. By God's grace I was able to forgive him and set him free in my heart.

I thank God for sparing my life so that I can bring the message of salvation and forgiveness to my broken people. I also thank God for the healing of my hurt and pain that I had endured for more than 25 years. Now, I can see the glory and experience the joy of serving him in my hometown.

Please pray for local Christians to stand up, to lead and to bring the message of salvation to their own people.

Update

Reconciliation

Since returning in June 2003 to the village where his family was killed, Reaksa has been able to raise funds to build a primary school there. This was dedicated in September 2004 as the symbol of forgiveness with the name of *"God's Grace Primary School Kokpreach"*.

Tragedy

In March 2004, Reaksa's brother-in-law (Chhunly Hourt) was robbed of his motorbike and his life while travelling near his home. Reaksa's sister, Sopheap, nephews and the whole family were shaken by this terrible tragedy. Reaksa wrote at the time, *"I have been hit by the storm so many times in my life, but this time, it is not a storm, but a typhoon. It is hard to take, especially to see my sister suffer. I thank God for calling me back to Cambodia to bring the message of salvation to Chhunly before he was called home to be with the Lord."*

Please pray that the family will see the rainbow through the rain.

Joy

Then on 4th February 2005 a daughter – Sophia Reaksa Himm – was born to Phaly and Reaksa. Reaksa writes, *"Years ago, when I was doing undergraduate study, I loved to study philosophy. The word "Philosophy" means the love of wisdom. I promised myself, that if I had children – a boy and a girl – I would name them Philos (love) for the boy and Sophia (wisdom) for the girl. The two together meaning philosophy – the love of wisdom. Now, my dream has come true."*

The journey continues.

GLOSSARY

Angkar	— organisation
Angkar loeu	— higher organisation
Bat, mith bong	— yes, comrade
Bong	— older brother or sister
Chao/chao proh	— grandson/granddaughter
Chlop	— secret agent/spy
Khmang	— enemy
Khmer Rouge	— Communist, Red Khmer
Kouy	— a different dialect of the Khmer language
Krama	— scarf
Kru Khmer	— shaman/witch doctor
Mak	— mother
Mith	— comrade
New-liberated people	— those who lived in the cities or outside the Khmer Rouge's zones before the country was liberated on 17th April 1975. Also called "April 17 people"
Old-liberated people	— those who lived in the Khmer Rouge's zones before the country was liberated on 17th April 1975
Pa or *papa*	— father
Pook	— father
Prothean phoum	— village leader
Reaksa	— protection
Reiy sontouch/ sontouch	— fishing/fishing lines
Santrane	— peace/peacefulness
Sent to school/ to study	— to be executed
Sok	— happiness
Ta or *tata*	— elder, elderly (male)

SAO CAMBODIA

On one of my recent visits to Cambodia, after lunch at the Phnom Penh Bible College where I had just spoken at the chapel hour, I was in conversation with Reaksa – one of the lecturers. He told me he had written his life story, but had yet to find a publisher. I was due to fly from Cambodia in an hour, so I asked if he had a copy of his manuscript. Thankfully he was able to oblige.

The long journey back to London passed quickly as I was riveted to my seat by his story. There was a sense of *déjà vu*, as my mind went back to 1980, talking with Cambodian refugees in the resettlement centre in Gravesend. Paul Penfold, the then Director of Cambodia for Christ, the forerunner of SAO Cambodia, had just been given the responsibility of managing the centre and was looking for ways to help the refugees cope with trauma by turning them to the comfort of the Christian scriptures.

In 1973, Paul with his wife Helen, had responded to an urgent plea from Major Chhirc Taing of the Cambodian military at Keswick Convention for prayer support. They undertook to gather names of those interested in praying for Cambodia. What would be more natural than to assist

Cambodian refugees arriving in the UK? This followed earlier steps to send volunteer workers into the refugee camps on the Cambodian/Thai border, which brought about the change of name to Southeast Asian Outreach.

Relationships with Cambodians were built in the camps and in this country. So that when in 1991 access to Cambodia itself became possible, SAO was one of the first NGOs to take up a government approved project. A fish farm project (called SCALE) was established, which today serves around 1,000 local farmers. It has spawned a small church outside Phnom Penh at its development centre.

In 2000, SAO Cambodia joined a consortium called International Co-operation Cambodia (ICC) and is now part of a team drawn from many nations working on a wide range of projects. One of those projects relates to trauma counselling as the nation still carries the wounds of the Pol Pot holocaust. For this reason and many others, SAO Cambodia is delighted and privileged to be able to join hands with Monarch Books in publishing this moving story of personal recovery and restoration to mark the mission's 30th Anniversary.

John Wallis, SAO Cambodia Trustee
January 2003

For further details about SAO Cambodia write to SAO Cambodia, Bawtry Hall, Bawtry, England DN10 6JH. E-mail: <admin@sao-cambodia.org> Web: <www.sao-cambodia.org>